Walking on Eggshells

Walking on Eggshells
Caring for a Critically Ill Loved One

By
Amy Sales, MSW, LCSW-C

New Horizon Press
Far Hills, NJ

Requests for permission should be addressed to:
New Horizon Press
P.O. Box 669
Far Hills, NJ 07931

Sales, Amy
Walking on Eggshells: Caring for a Critically Ill Loved One

Cover design: Robert Aulicino
Interior design: Susan Sanderson

Library of Congress Control Number: 2011928842

ISBN 13: 978-0-88282-380-5
New Horizon Press

Manufactured in the U.S.A.

16   15   14   13   12   1   2   3   4   5

TO

*Nikki, who held my hand along the way
and unconditionally loved me
through the highs and lows of this process;
my beautiful daughter, Madison, who teaches me every day
that you can never love a child too much;
and to my family and friends for all of their endless support.*

Author's Note

This book is based on the author's research, personal and work experiences and clients' real-life experiences. Unless permissions were granted, the names and identifying characteristics of the cases and people in this book have been altered to ensure confidentiality. Only the names of contributing experts remain.

For purposes of simplifying usage, the pronouns he/she and him/her are sometimes used interchangeably. The information contained herein is not meant to be a substitute for professional evaluation and therapy with mental health professionals.

Contents

❧ Introduction ❧

All too often it is not until we face a loved one's critical illness, truly a life-altering event, that we reflect on and do a mental inventory of our relationship with him or her. The fact that you are reading this book may indicate that you are experiencing such an event right now. It is natural to feel frightened and perhaps overwhelmed by arduous and daunting tasks and the needs of your loved one as you both face this difficult and emotional time.

This book is intended for you, the caregiver. The caregiver plays a unique and vital role for a loved one who has a life-threatening disease. It is my hope that as you read you will find comfort, helpful guidelines and a sense of direction for the uncharted journey that you are about to take.

The information and advice in this book will let you know that you are not alone in your day-to-day role as the silent hero and allow you to look back later with a feeling of peace and lack of regret.

I have been providing counseling on the emotional aspects of terminal illnesses and grief to patients and their caregivers for more than twenty years. I have come to understand the significance of "making the most out of each day" and "not to put off for tomorrow what can be done today." I am blessed to be employed in a profession that reminds me each day that life is too short and to appreciate the gifts lying in front of me, no matter how big or small.

In my counseling, I have met with many individuals who have taken a lifetime to connect with these gifts. Unfortunately, I have also encountered others who were never able to do this.

It is common to struggle with what to do or say when your loved one is facing a life-threatening disease. Many people feel as though they are "walking on eggshells." I have witnessed many missed opportunities to reach out and show support to those who are very ill due to the fear of saying the wrong words or the inability to find words at all.

Throughout this book I will provide useful advice, strategies, information and examples in order to make reaching out to a terminally ill loved one less frightening. I know from long experience that you will become aware of many instances throughout this journey when the "eggshells" of difficult experiences are present and how hard it can be to make your way forward when they occur on the path you must navigate.

I will share what I have experienced as common themes and problems that patients, families and caregivers encounter. Taking on the role of caregiver does not come with a set of instructions. Rather, it is based on love and commitment. Be gentle with yourself as you read onward and as you embark on this arduous journey.

ᕙ Chapter 1 ᕗ

Life after the Diagnosis

Life will not be the same as you and your family knew it prior to receiving the diagnosis of a life-threatening illness. Your first role as caregiver and support system is to be aware that your loved one will experience a range of emotions. You may, at times, find that your own feelings will change in tandem with his or hers. At other times, the two of you may be in very different places emotionally.

Your job is to be tuned in to the ill person's emotions and to recognize when to reach out and help calm or ground him or her. From this point forward, you must expect the unexpected.

Nobody ever knows how he or she will respond when given a life-threatening illness diagnosis. Shock and disbelief are feelings many experience. Here are a few typical reactions I have seen in the patients whom I and other caregivers have encountered:

- "This can't be right."
- "I must be in a bad dream."
- "No, this is not happening to me."

When the majority of people receive diagnoses of life-threatening illnesses, they become instantly frightened and assume their diagnoses mean death. It is not until the patients discuss the diagnoses with their physicians and hear treatment options with clear plans of action that they can take a deep breath and feel a sense of hope.

When I meet with a patient, I explain to him or her that he or she is on the roller coaster of his or her life. There will be highs, lows and in-betweens. The ride may change from minute to minute and is not predictable. But I assure the patient, just as you will as a caregiver, that he or she will not be on the ride alone.

Patients and their caregivers share a common condition from the minute the diagnosis is received: immense loss of control. I cannot think of a greater feeling of loss of control for both parties. Patients would do anything to protect their loved ones from having to imagine life without them and caregivers would do anything to make their loved ones well.

Many of us feel we have to be in control of our lives, family, relationships and health at all times. The ultimate feeling of loss of control comes when we face our own mortality. Imagine the anxiety that your loved one must be experiencing at this time. It is important to understand that many patients lose their sense of identity while fighting for their lives. Many are not able to work, provide for their families, take care of their loved ones or perform their daily routines independently. These are experiences which take away all the confidence we have learned to value in building our lives.

In providing support for you, the caregiver, I will help you refocus your feelings of helplessness into simple yet powerful actions that will also help your loved one maintain control. Throughout this journey I encourage you to ask yourself, *What can I do to give him or her a sense of more control?* There is always something right in front of you.

My experience has taught me to allow people who have life-threatening illnesses to have as much control as possible. It may be as simple as giving them what they want to eat or as complicated as getting a second, third or fourth expert medical opinion on their conditions. Your loved one must be able to make choices that fit his or her needs. I am referring to patients who are of sound mind, who have good judgment and who are not placing themselves in unsafe situations.

You may not always agree with the choices that your terminally ill loved one will make. I hope that your relationship provides opportunities to discuss things "as a team." But if he or she is sound enough to make choices, whether you agree or not, try to keep in mind that this is someone who is very much trying to regain some sense of control. The role of the caregiver will often be to support the wishes and needs of a loved one who is doing everything possible to maintain "normal," when everything in his or her life seems anything but normal.

Topics for Reflection

1. What have been your prominent feelings since your loved one was diagnosed? Are you feeling loss of control? Remember, this is the most common feeling experienced by caregivers and the goal is to help you regain some control, which will allow you to be available for your loved one.

2. Can you think of things that you can do to regain some control after reading this chapter? Make a list of what is feeling completely out of your control right now (it can consist of simple or complicated things) and then make a list of possible ways to gain some control over them (e.g., solicit family and friends to help with the children, meals or mowing the grass). It's better to regain some control where you can rather than to feel overwhelmed by everything.

3. How is your loved one coping with the diagnosis? Try to imagine the range of emotions that your loved one must be feeling. If his or her behaviors and/or moods do not reflect what you are experiencing as a caregiver, that is okay. Everyone copes with stress differently and he or she may need some space to absorb the reality of the situation.

4. How can you give your ill loved one some sense of control during this time period? Everyone's answer is different, but I encourage you to place some thought into finding some simple yet powerful ways to achieve this. For example, ask him or her if he or she is satisfied with the treatment options or if he or she would prefer to get a second

and/or third opinion. Perhaps your loved one would like to have the family over to break the news or take a short trip with you to think things through. Whether or not you are ready for certain things isn't the issue; instead, you are trying to support your loved one with tasks that may bring some calmness to a chaotic situation.

Chapter 2

When Finding the Right Words Seems Impossible

Have you ever spent several minutes looking all over the refrigerator for one particular item, only to discover that it was right in front of you on the top shelf the entire time? We have all done it. Then we wonder, *How could I have missed what was directly in front of me?*

People often tell me, "I wanted to call him, because I heard he was sick, but I didn't, because I was scared that I wouldn't know what to say or that I would say the wrong thing." It is difficult learning that someone you care for has a life-threatening disease. Under these circumstances, it is normal to be at a loss for words, but I want to point out to you that the words you are seeking are "on the shelf" directly in front of you.

Here is an example of comforting words to say to your loved one, whether it's in person, on the phone, left on an answering machine or electronic device or written in an e-mail or greeting card:

> I am so sorry to hear that you are sick. I wish that I knew the right words to make it better, but I don't. I want you to know that I am here for you and I will continue to keep you in my thoughts and my heart. I don't want you to feel compelled to talk if you don't want to, so I won't keep you. But should you need anything or just want to talk, please know that you can call me anytime.

Simply let the person know that you are aware, concerned and available. Furthermore, provide him or her space by not "pushing" and at the same time offering the assurance that you will continue to be there should he or she need you.

Some caregivers make the mistake of suggesting that everything will be okay. Our hurt and pain make it tempting to be overly hopeful when there may be no real information that the patient will get better and to say things such as: "You will fight this and be cured." The power of positive thinking can at times be very important; however, such words may be of no help to the person who has a major illness and, in fact, may not even be realistic.

Imagine for a few moments what you might feel like if a doctor just told you that you have a life-threatening disease. What is your first emotion? I would venture to guess that sheer panic comes to your mind. Another common reaction is shock and disbelief.

If you have children, you probably have experienced what I call "panic mode" at least once. For instance: You are at a public place with your child and turn your head to look at something for a second. When you turn back around, you do not see your child. Your heart races, your tunnel vision is acutely searching/scanning, you cannot hear the noises around you that were there only a moment ago and you're already fearing that your child is lost. When you spot your child who wandered off, you can feel the rush of blood and oxygen re-entering your body.

But what if you had to continue to live and function in that state of fright? That's how a person feels when told he or she has a life-threatening diagnosis.

This relates to knowing what to say to your ill loved one. If you attempt to identify with his or her feelings, the words will be easier to find. It will also sound genuine and sincere. Here are some other examples of what you can say to a loved one facing a life-threatening illness:

- "I am sorry that you are sick."
- "I feel really bad."
- "If you need anything, I am here."

- "We are going to do this together. I do not want you to feel alone."
- "I don't want to push if you don't feel like talking. Would you rather that I give you some space?"
- "What can I do to help you?"
- "You must be experiencing so many emotions. I'm happy to listen if you want to share."
- "I am not sure what to say, but I wanted to tell you that I am thinking about you and carrying you with me in my heart."

There are many people who will still have a difficult time reaching out to their seriously ill loved ones, despite their strong urge to do so. For these people I suggest buying a greeting card and writing: "I am thinking about you." You may view it as a simple gesture, but I assure you that the person who receives it will find it comforting.

It is my impression that many people shy away from offering support, because they are afraid that there will be a period of awkward silence between their loved ones and themselves. Through my experience I have found that the power of presence is more potent than you could ever imagine. Oftentimes, no words at all are needed to convey that you care and share another's pain. Just being there provides support and love.

Topics for Reflection

1. Are you feeling hesitant and unsure about reaching out to your critically ill loved one? If so, explore what may be holding you back (fear, anxiety, not knowing what to say, etc.).

2. What has been your method of communicating with your loved one prior to his or her becoming sick? If this wasn't a strong point in the relationship, I encourage you to step out of your comfort zone and take some risks with telling your loved one how you feel. Remember, it can be as simple as saying it in a card.

3. What do you imagine that your loved one's reaction will be to your words of comfort? Do you feel equipped to handle his or her reaction, whatever that may be?

$\backsim$ Chapter 3 $\backsim$

Who to Tell What
and When to Tell It

When is the right time to tell others that your loved one is critically ill? Depending on to whom you talk, the answer will differ based on personalities and preferences. I have met many individuals who share their diagnoses with everyone and others who do not tell anyone. As every individual has different needs and styles, I cannot recommend whether or not to share the difficult situation of your loved one's life-threatening illness, but I will provide you with information from my many years of experience with terminally ill patients and their caregivers that may help you make your choice. Also, I will give you suggestions to aid you and your loved one in coping with these decisions.

I am a firm believer that there are no "shoulds" or "should nots." In other words, many people do what they think they *should* and compromise their true desires: "I *should* call my friends and tell them I am sick, because they will be hurt if I do not." This can lead to resentment.

When someone you love is very ill, you may feel it would be selfish to honor your own needs. However, I want to remind you to put your needs first! Share information when the time feels right. Your desire to inform or update people will shift over time. Good news is easy to deliver; bad news can be more difficult.

I believe there is one exception to whether or not to share the diagnosis: If you have children, I strongly encourage you share information without delay. I will address this issue in more detail in the next chapter. For now, let's focus on whether or not to share information with friends, family or employers.

Employers and Colleagues

If you, the caregiver, are employed, I think that it is important to provide some information to your employer. Because of your loved one's needs, medical treatment and condition, your life will not be predictable and you need the support of your employer. Many employers show compassion and understanding when they are notified that an employee's loved one is ill. They may respond by saying, "I completely understand, take whatever time you need." Others may be stricter.

Nonetheless, a person's job may be at risk. The work still has to get done. Ask your employer whether or not this is something about which you need to be worried. Determine with your employer the limits to how much time you may take off.

Your ill loved one may miss workdays due to treatment sessions and side effects. The amount of time off will differ from person to person, depending on what type of illness he or she has. I suggest that you share my recommendations with your loved one, because you both need to seek out this information. This is a topic on which I am very insistent. Neither of you can plan and make choices without guidelines. You both may be nervous or hesitant to ask these questions of your employers, but it is necessary. Finances are a big concern when it comes to worries during illness. Find out soon what your options are.

After you obtain this information, you will be able to organize better. If you have a strong external support system, you may need others to take turns accompanying your loved one to appointments or watching your children, so you can go to work. I will address benefits through employers in a later chapter. Right now, I am focused on helping you determine who to tell and why some people are more important than others when it comes to taking care of your needs and responsibilities and attending to your own well-being.

Friends and Family Members

Let's discuss whether or not to tell friends and family members. I want to share something with you: The secret is that there is no secret at all. This means that once you tell one friend or family member, whether you like it or not the news will spread. This is what humans do. It is just too difficult to expect people to keep this kind of information to themselves. I have found that this type of news doesn't get passed on as a form of gossip but, rather, out of concern. Be gentle with your best friend or family member who swore that he or she would not share but then broke the promise. Make it easier for your friends and family by explaining that you'd rather they keep the news about your loved one's illness confidential for now but that you understand if they need to share.

Each person's needs are different, so follow your gut and heart. I recommend that you tell people (friends, family, important colleagues) for several reasons:

- Keeping secrets can be a source of stress and take up energy.
- The support that these people can provide can be extremely helpful.
- It is important that you know that you are not alone on this journey.

There is a common reason that prevents many of us from sharing information: We feel uneasy receiving. If you ask people whether or not they feel more comfortable giving or receiving from others, the majority will answer giving.

Receiving makes most of us uncomfortable and embarrassed. Some of this feeling can be traced back to a person's first childhood birthday party. All eyes were on you to perform, smile, appreciate and reward those who gave to you with hugs, kisses and "thank yous." And it was all fun and games until your teenage years. Around this time, instead of performing, you wanted to crawl into a shell during a gathering that was for you. To make things worse, your face turned beet red, because all eyes were on you once again and hugging your aunt just wasn't what it used to be. Receiving became stressful. We learned creative ways to avoid and/or rush through the process.

Learning to accept from others is an art. It takes skill, practice and talent. There is a right way to receive and a wrong way. Learning how to navigate walking on eggshells is tricky.

The minute you tell others that you or your loved one is very ill, they want to discuss or give advice. First the questions come at you: "What can I do? What do you need? How can I help? Can I watch your children for you? Can I bring you meals? Can I drive you to appointments? Can I have a fundraiser in your name?" These are wonderful gestures that you may not be ready yet to accept.

Often I hear patients say, "I have always provided for myself and my family. I do not want to be a charity case." Here are some other reactions:

- "I don't want to be a burden."
- "I have always paid my bills and don't want to be viewed as someone who needs to be on welfare."
- "I can drive myself to appointments."
- "My adult children are not supposed to be taking care of me."

You and your loved one did not ask or invite this illness into your lives, but people love and care about you. Reflect on these questions for a while:

- If the situation were reversed, would you be reaching out to help those who want to help you now?
- Would you feel that they are a burden to you?
- Would you be seeking gratitude or paybacks?
- Would you bring them a meal or send them a card?
- Would you feel that watching their children is the least you could do?
- Would you gladly place money in an envelope for them, with no name to indicate who gave it?
- Would you take them to an appointment?

- Would you think less of them because they have a disease and need as many supports as possible to carry them through?
- Would you sit with them in a quiet room just to keep them company?
- Would you give them a hug, because your heart feels the urge?

These actions and reactions are ones that many of us would offer to others and are good reasons to allow your friends and family to help now, so welcome their gestures. If people are reaching out to you to help, it is a compliment to you as a person. I imagine that you are getting back what you've given.

In the future, you will probably come across someone else with whom you will have an opportunity to "pay it forward." Take mental notes now and learn to pass on certain things to the next person who will need to receive rather than give. The greatest gift that you can give to other human beings is to allow them to give to you; the reward for them isn't measured in anything other than their hearts.

After you share your news with family and friends, keeping in touch with everyone may feel overwhelming. Here are some suggestions for maintaining order after sharing the news your loved one is ill:

- Set boundaries and explain to people that it will be too difficult to talk about everything on a regular basis. Let them know that you appreciate their support and will update them as your energy permits.
- Many patients and their families create Web sites or blogs or send mass e-mails in order to update the people they care about. You can design Web pages (e.g., CarePages.com) that can provide medical updates. It gets exhausting to give the same updates over and over to others. Place your needs first. This is not the time for being a "people pleaser" or to worry about hurting others' feelings if you don't return calls. However, you should take the time (when you have some) to express that you appreciate their concern.

- Remember, it may have taken a lot of courage for them to reach out to you. Don't ignore others' kind gestures; acknowledge them with warmth and provide information as to how you will share updates. People will be holding you in their hearts and they will be feeling helpless. Allow them to receive updates (e.g., via e-mail) and to send you messages filled with support.
- If updating through technology feels overwhelming, that is okay. Some people appoint a close friend or relative to do this for them on a regular basis. Delegate where you can.

During this difficult time, your needs *must* come first. Your friends and family will understand.

Topics for Reflection

1. Would you characterize yourself as generally open or secretive? Are you comfortable speaking to others about your personal life and that of your loved one?

2. Both your job and your loved one's may be at risk. It is important to provide some information to employers in order to gain their support and clarify the situation.

3. If you share the situation with a friend or family member, the news will spread quickly. Don't expect them to keep it to themselves.

4. Remember, if you have children, I strongly encourage you to share this information with them as soon as possible.

$\backsim$ Chapter 4 $\backsim$

Talking to Your Children about Terminal Illness and Dying

No matter what age children are (three or thirty years old), it is parents' hope to protect them. To watch our children struggle and hurt is probably one of the most difficult things that parents experience. I approach this topic not only as a parent, but also as a clinician who has provided support to many parents on how to present information about the life-threatening illness of a loved one to their children.

Unfortunately, there will be times when we as parents will not be able to make things "all better" and our jobs will shift from protectors to supporters. My heart truly goes out to you and your terminally ill loved one as you proceed to talk with your children. I also want to convey to you that there is no right or wrong way to talk to them. The most important thing is that you talk.

This chapter covers material from the first day of diagnosis through the possibility of death. You may find it emotionally difficult to read, but I am attempting to set a foundation for difficult situations that you may have to face in the future.

Showing Emotions

Many parents don't talk to their children about life-threatening diagnoses, because they are afraid to show their emotions. I want you to refocus that thought to this: A parent's job is to be a life-long coach. You are teaching and modeling for your children and the greatest coaches are those who model the skills that will benefit their players to play a successful game.

Crying in front of your children doesn't make you a weak person. The myth that "we must stay strong" for our children is simply that: a myth. Children are smart and intuitive. Whether you share information with them or not, they will know instinctively that something is not normal in your house. As much as you may think that you can hide your stress and anxiety from them, you can't. Children know their parents and their moods better than parents would ever imagine.

The emotions that you exhibit in front of your children serve several purposes:

- That it is okay and normal to show emotions.
- That they are not alone and can share with you.
- That you too have feelings.

Children need to learn to be compassionate to others; what better place to start than at home?

Sharing Information about the Diagnosis

Not sharing information with children only makes the monster in the closet one hundred times scarier than talking about reality.

Imagine yourself as a child with one or both of your parents constantly going to doctor appointments. Furthermore, you hear your parents whispering information on the phone or between themselves. Children are alert to secrets; when you think that they are not listening, they are.

Experience has taught me that it is easier to understand children's perceptions and how they experience these situations if they are grouped according to age and development stage. There is a wealth of literature available that discusses and defines development stages of children and I encourage you to explore it if you want to learn more. Meanwhile, I would like to share with you what others have found helpful and let you determine what is a good fit for you and your child.

I have divided the age groups based on my experience, but if these divisions don't seem appropriate for your child, go to the prior or following age group. No matter what age your child is, much of the information in the Under Twelve Months category relates to all ages.

Under Twelve Months

Children have not acquired effective language skills at this age and their ability to receive and send messages about a parent's illness is next to impossible. Here's what they do understand: They know if there has been a shift in your availability and mood. Furthermore, if you become physically or emotionally withdrawn, they will feel the change. I know it is easier said than done during a time of crisis, but remind yourself on a regular basis to take necessary time to be "present" with your child.

Ages One through Four

At this stage children start to become more verbal and aware of the world around them. Their ability to sense that something is wrong has continued to advance and they will feel your stress despite your efforts to hide it. Communicating with children this young can be challenging; my suggestion is to keep it very basic and simple. For example, you can say something like:

> Daddy is sick. His body has a booboo inside it and he
> is going to a doctor who is trying to make him feel bet-
> ter. The medicine may take a while to work and Daddy
> might be tired and need to take a lot of naps. Daddy
> and I love you very much. Do you have any questions?

There usually is no need to expand on the dialogue any further. Your child will most likely go back to his or her own pursuits and you have created a foundation on which future conversations can be built.

Ages Five through Seven

Around age five, children begin to ask questions about death. Usually it begins with a question related to a dead bug or animal. Death is very confusing to them and providing answers can be challenging. Parents have different and unique ways of answering these questions. It is important to know that the world becomes more complex around age five. Children's ability to communicate and receive information improves dramatically at this point, yet they are still very concrete and require information to be stated in simple terms. To a child in this age group you might say something such as:

> Mommy has not been feeling well so she went to the doctor and he said that she is sick. He is going to give her some medicine which we hope will make her better. She will need to keep going to the doctor so he can see how she is doing. Because Mommy has not been feeling well she may take naps during the day. The medicine that Mommy will be taking may make her hair fall out. Can you think of anyone that we know who doesn't have hair? I bet you can use your imagination and draw a picture of what Mommy will look like without hair. It might make you sad that Mommy will not be able to play as much if she is tired. We both love you very much and you and I will have special playtime too.

It is possible that your child may ask you if the ill parent is going to die. Remember that this is the stage when children begin to learn about death and to question whether or not their parents will die.

Answers to these questions differ from parent to parent. Here is an example of what you could say:

> We are all going to die one day and some people die sooner than others. Mommy and I hope to live for a long time and that is why Mommy is going to the doctor, because he is trying to make her illness go away. You and I will talk about it if Mommy doesn't get better.

Be prepared; you will now receive many additional questions, because your child's mind will be racing to gather information. Keep your answers flowing, but make sure that they are not too scary or too detailed. When children sense that something is wrong, it is only natural that they will look for the "scary monster in the closet." If you provide them with information, that monster doesn't have to be so scary.

Children need to feel part of the process. Give them tasks to do so they feel involved (e.g., draw pictures for Mommy, bring a drink to Mommy, help Daddy clean up, feed the dog, etc.). Keep them involved on a daily basis, so they feel included instead of excluded.

Ages Eight through Twelve

This is the time when children often still like their parents and their need for separation and a sense of self is not the primary agenda. It is during these years that children continue to rely on direction and boundaries from their parents as they improve their social skills and increase their involvement in structured activities. Children in this age group also continue to advance in their ability to understand the concept of death and are able to engage in conversations about their feelings and emotions as they relate to having a seriously ill parent and/or enduring a loss.

Each child is different in his or her level of maturity, but most children ages eight to twelve will be able to handle the news that a parent has a life-limiting illness. Provide your child with information and allow the time and space for questions. Keep the information basic and factual, but there is no need to dilute it, because your child will see through your attempts to protect him or her. Children in this age category *are* capable of handling the stressors that accompany the unfortunate circumstances that surround them. Reassure your child that you are healthy and you are not going to leave him or her. Give your child support, create open communication and remember that you are a life coach. Your child is looking to you for direction and examples for how to conduct him or herself during difficult times.

Here are examples of how to discuss terminal illness with a child in this age range:

- As you know, your mother hasn't been feeling well for a few months and the test results show that she has breast cancer. I know that this sounds scary, but there is reason to believe right now that she can be cured with the medicines that are available. Our lives will be a little upside down for a while and your mother and I are here anytime to answer your questions or just to give hugs.

- It may be difficult to concentrate in school right now and I want to reassure you that your father is receiving the best medical care possible. His job is to fight this disease while yours is to try to stay focused on your schoolwork and activities. We will update you with information as we learn it and together, as a family, we will face this.

Make sure to alert your child's school counselors of current events so they can assist in monitoring your child for behavior changes. Children in this age range may migrate to their friends for support or may regress and become needier of your time and attention. Both are normal reactions. Despite age and maturity, a scared child may still continue to need you to remain in control and to guide him or her along the way.

Teenagers

It can be very difficult to navigate discussing a sick parent with teens. I think that it will make a difference whether your teenager is male or female, because different sexes usually exhibit different emotions.

Teenagers' brains are moving through thoughts quickly; they are trying to figure out their identities and, most importantly, how to separate from their parents. All of this is normal, expected and must take place in order for them to emerge into adulthood with a healthy sense of self.

It is important that you identify what is normal behavior for your teenager (e.g., moody, irritable or embarrassed to be seen with you), because he or she may become even more unpredictable when faced with a parent's illness.

You must be honest and direct with your teen about what is going on and although he or she may not appear to be interested, he or she really is. Many teens are not good at expressing their feelings and may feel resentful if you "push" them to talk. Let your teenager know that you are available and will make the time to answer questions and talk whenever he or she has the need. Allow your teen to see you express feelings and show him or her your humanness and vulnerability. Keep in mind that though your teen may not look like a toddler any longer, he or she will still need to know that you are in control and are available for support. No matter what your child's age or how he or she feels about the situation, hugging is beneficial.

Here is an example of how to begin a discussion with a teenager:

> I know that Dad's illness is scary and that our lives
> have been turned upside down. We will all have to
> work together as a family to get through this. I under-
> stand if you are angry or resentful. If we could change
> the situation, we would. But in the meantime I will
> do everything possible to help maintain a normal
> schedule and not interrupt your activities. Although I
> can't make any promises right now, I care very much
> about your feelings and how you are doing. Let's try
> to check in with each other on a regular basis, so I am
> aware of what your needs are too. If you ever want to
> talk, I am here to listen.

Teens live in a world of entitlement. It is okay to set limits and boundaries if they expect that their world should not be interfered with. It is your job as a parent to provide "teachable" moments. Compassion, concern and selflessness are required life tools and there is no better time than the present circumstances to model and teach these skills to your teen.

It is common that teens will turn to friends rather than their parents for support. They also may become angry or withdrawn. My suggestion to you is not to second-guess your teenager's methods for coping and provide him or her space (as long as he or she is not placing him or herself into any harm). On the other hand, if your teen's mood or actions change dramatically, it could be a call for help. Follow your gut and reach out when your intuition kicks in.

Adult Children

It is my hope that by now your child has matured, encountered some life lessons and can cope more effectively with difficult situations. You should be honest and direct about what is going on, the expected treatment plan and how you and your ill loved one are feeling. Many parents have the need to protect their children from bad news. Countless times I have heard parents say, "I do not want to call my children, because I don't want to upset or worry them."

I suggest reflecting on this question: How would you feel if your son or daughter withheld information from you for the same reasons?

I know our job as parents is to protect our children from discomfort and pain whenever possible. I do not believe that theory applies to this situation. You are a family unit in good times and bad. That is the magic of a family. It is the greatest support system you will ever encounter, because it is unconditional. Withholding information doesn't protect children; it excludes them. It denies you the care and support that they have to offer and most importantly, it will make them question whether or not they can trust that you will share in the future. It also requires more energy to keep it from them when you need whatever energy you can preserve right now.

I want to caution you about keeping the boundaries clear. You are the parent and he or she is the child, even as an adult. The family members will support one another during this difficult time, but you need to remain in the parental role. I have witnessed the roles reverse in many situations as adult children took over the parental duties, both physically and emotionally. They became full-time caregivers, supporters and spokespersons. This is not and should not be their responsibility. You and your partner (whatever the nature of your relationship) are the captains of the ship and you need to direct and support the crew.

Allow your adult child to be a part of the process. He or she will probably feel the need to contribute and being involved is probably his or her way of having some sense of control. Let your son or daughter help. Your job is to make sure that your adult child knows it is okay to continue to live his or her own life as well.

One last suggestion: They are never too grown up to need your hugs!

Discussing Death

Talking to your children prior to your loved one's death and explaining what death looks like will open the door for useful conversations. It will also begin to prepare them for what is ahead emotionally. These conversations may be painful for you. But know that your children will be able to handle this, because they have you to hug. If you try to avoid these difficult conversations now, you are not protecting them, only delaying the inevitable. Allow them to hear the information from you, because you love them unconditionally, as opposed to people outside the situation who may not be so understanding.

Tailor your conversation based on your children's ages and developmental stages, but no matter the age be sure to use the word *die*. It is vital that you don't sugarcoat the meaning of death in order to protect your children from the emotional pain. This may be their first time having to deal with this concept, but, unfortunately, death is a reality of life and they need to begin to develop coping skills.

This situation is more difficult for you emotionally and figuring out what to say to your children may feel overwhelming. Here is an example of what you may want to say in order to handle this very sad and trying time:

> Remember when Daddy and I explained to you
> that he has cancer and that the doctors were doing
> everything possible to make him feel better? I wish
> that I could tell you that he is all better, but he isn't.
> The doctors have tried all the medicine that they can,
> but Daddy's illness is getting worse. Daddy is going
> to die.

When you are explaining what death looks like, be mindful of the words that you use. People commonly make the mistake of describing death as looking like someone is sleeping. We think that we are protecting children by making death appear peaceful, but instead this message can create fear. A child may become frightened to go to sleep, because if that is what death "looks like," he may think that he will not wake up.

Here is a suggestion of how you could explain death:

> Johnny, as you know, Daddy is really sick with cancer
> and he has tried really hard to get better, but he
> isn't able to. The doctors said that he is going to die.
> Daddy's body is really tired and when he dies his
> heart will stop beating. He will not be breathing, his
> skin color will become paler and he will feel cold if
> you touch him.

Here is a poor example of explaining the death of a parent:

> Daddy will go to a better place when he dies. He will
> be up in heaven looking over you.

A child may then have a strong desire to die so he can be with his Daddy and in a "better place."

A better choice may be:

> When Daddy dies his spirit will leave his body. That
> spirit will continue to live in your heart and surround
> you forever.

It will be helpful to you, as the parent, to reminisce and share fond stories of your loved one with your children. This keeps his or her spirit alive and it also reassures your children that it is not taboo to talk about someone who is gone.

I know it is difficult to have these discussions. It is okay for you to show emotion during these conversations, because, remember, you are modeling to your children that emotions are normal and acceptable. Parents are real people and they cry and get sad too. Just choose your words carefully to make sure that your children don't feel like they have to be *your* caregiver.

Your children will need time to process the information you provide. Discussing death is not a one-time incident. Just as you will experience shifts in emotions, so will your children. Make time to "check in" with your children and to let them know you are available to listen and talk.

Children have a difficult time putting their feelings into words. If you ask, "How are you feeling?" do not be surprised if you get a short answer. I suggest presenting your question like this: "I feel sad that Daddy is sick and going to die. It makes me feel a little better when I cry. Are you sad too?" In this example you are normalizing your child's feelings and using yourself as an example. As life moves forward, try to be conscious to continue to make time to "check in."

Reassure Your Child that You Are Not Going Anywhere

Losing a parent is frightening to a child. It is beyond comprehension to many children that their parents could be permanently gone, so imagine what feelings arise when a parent does die. Perhaps the child is thinking, *If Daddy dies, then will Mommy die too?*

Reassure your child that you will not die now also. I know you are probably leery to promise to your child that you are not going to die yet, because unfortunately accidents and illness as well as crime victimization can happen to anyone at any moment. Yes, that is true, but the odds of it happening soon are very slim. However, many children who face losing one parent have tremendous fear about losing the other parent too.

When speaking to a child who fears losing both parents, you might say something such as:

> I know that you are sad and scared that Daddy is
> going to die. I promise you that I am not dying too.
> In fact, I plan to stick around for a long, long time to
> take care of you.

You may be questioning why I use the word *promise* in that example. We are taught early in life not to make promises that we can't keep. This is one of those situations where I believe you can make a promise and gamble with the odds. Children place a lot of weight on the word *promise* and they *need* to know that you will be staying around.

If your child follows this with a question such as, "Are you going to live forever?"it is okay to be honest. You may want to reply with something like this: "Everybody is going to die. Nobody lives forever, but I hope to live to be a very old woman."

It is also appropriate to use humor to lighten up the mood. For example, "I am expecting to live to be an old woman, so I can hug and tickle your children too."

Modeling Self-Care

It is important to model, through both words and actions, healthy self-care for children. You can say something such as: "I hope to live to a very old age. That is why I take sixty minutes a day to exercise. That is also why I try to watch what I eat and go to my doctor for regular check-ups."

If you are not currently following healthy self-care, here is my wake-up call to you. Start taking care of yourself if you aren't! Exercise, eat healthy foods and take time to relax and de-stress. It will make you feel so much better.

Helping Your Children Say Goodbye

Children need to be included in their family activities and plans when a parent is dying. Continue to delegate tasks to children to keep them involved. Here are some other ways to include your child in the final stages of your loved one's life. Encourage him or her to:

- Read a book with the ill parent.
- Draw pictures or create other artwork for the ill parent.
- Buy or make a special present (e.g., a stuffed animal) for the ill parent.
- Make a card to give to the ill parent.

If your loved one is no longer conscious, explain to your children: "Daddy is not able to open his eyes and talk to you now, because his illness makes him sleep a lot. But his mind knows that you are present."

Let your children know that if they want to talk to the unconscious parent, hold his or her hand or just sit in the room, they can. Try not to push any of these options, though. Allow your children to do what feels comfortable for them and give them permission to exit a visit at any time should they feel the need to.

Determining the Best Care for Your Dying Loved One When Children Are Present

Many caregivers are unsure how to handle the situation of a dying loved one when children are present. Is it better to keep the ill parent at home or to utilize a facility? I want to remind you that I do not believe in "shoulds" or "should nots" (e.g., I *should* relocate my loved one into a facility, because my extended family thinks it's wrong to allow the children to see him dying).

Follow your heart and your gut, which is certainly *much* easier said than done. Here is a chart of things to consider which may help you sort through this complicated question and find what works best for you and your family.

This comparative table will allow you to explore the realistic issues that help people make these kinds of decisions. As stated before, your loved one's safety has to be number one on the priority list. If both options are available to you (at home or in a facility) but it is difficult to make a decision, I will share my preference based on what I have witnessed: I have had many people ask to have their loved ones transferred to inpatient facilities days before they pass away, because they wanted to protect the children. I have also seen a similar number keep their loved ones home for the duration.

REALISTIC TO BE AT HOME	UNREALISTIC TO BE AT HOME
I have enough support in my home to assist with the children.	I have very little support and will need to be a full-time caretaker to my loved one and my children.
I can handle the 24/7 medical needs that my loved one will require.	
Financial issues are not a concern and I don't have to work right now.	My loved one's medical needs are too complex and I can't keep him or her safe.
I can hire an aide to assist with my loved one's needs.	I have to work.
I can have home hospice set up, because there will be 24/7 caregivers in my home.	I can't afford to hire an aide.
Emotionally I cannot handle having my loved one die at home, but I want to keep him there as long as possible.	Home hospice is not appropriate, because nobody can stay at home to provide caregiving.
Hospice care can provide emotional support to my children in the home.	My children will experience seeing their parent in pain or having difficult treatments in their own home, which can cause awful memories.
Hospice will assist with getting my loved one into a facility when the time comes so that my children don't experience his dying at home as a last memory.	
I can place my loved one into an inpatient hospice setting and not pursue home hospice, because it will be too difficult for me and the children emotionally and physically.	

You may be experiencing guilt if it is not an option to have your loved one in the home at all. Please replace that feeling with this idea: You are not "putting" your loved one away. You are taking care of him or her by making sure that his or her needs as well as your children's are taken care of. That is the greatest act of love possible. It is when you forsake your loved one's needs out of guilt that you run a greater risk of having regrets.

Here are some points to keep in mind while discussing terminal illnesses and death with your children:

- Children sense the stress and sadness that parents are feeling. The secrets and the unknown become much scarier to them, because their imaginations look for "monsters" when unfamiliar negative feelings are present.
- Keeping information from your children takes much more energy out of you than you have to spare right now.
- Children often get "pushed to the side" when adults are experiencing stress. This creates a strong sense of aloneness for them, when the main people who are supposed to be available to provide comfort are often seen to go "missing."
- Remember that the role you took on by becoming a parent is similar to acting as a lifelong coach. You will model and teach important life skills in good times and bad. Furthermore, an effective coach draws out the best in a person and teaches how to cope and remain resilient in the hardest of times.

Over the years I have come to realize that there is no right or wrong way to handle talking to children about death and dying. You know your family's needs better than anyone else. Focus on what's best for you, your loved one and the children.

Topics for Reflection

1. What are your strengths and weaknesses when communicating with your children? Have you and your loved one shared the diagnosis and

other age-appropriate information with them yet? If you haven't, I strongly encourage you to begin to include them, if old enough, in the process.

2.   If you have already shared with them, how did that conversation go? Was it one of the most painful conversations that you have ever had to experience? Did you feel helpless? If the answers to these questions are "yes," then you are experiencing what many parents do when talking to their children about this topic. I applaud your efforts and ask that you keep the lines of communication open.

3.   Are you unable to communicate with your children due to fear and anxiety? If the answer is "yes", this too is common and I encourage seeking additional help from school counselors, therapists or family/ friends to help initiate discussion with your children.

4.   Did you share what is going on with your children only to be met with no reaction at all? If so, your children may need to time to absorb and process what was said. Give them some space and revisit the topic in a day or two.

Chapter 5

How to Prepare for Medical Appointments

You are embarking on the complex tasks of taking on the roles of advocate, team leader, interpreter, gatekeeper, counselor, cheerleader, boxing bag and hugger. When things are out of sync in our lives, it becomes difficult to manage our everyday routines, let alone understand and organize what is said and recommended by a physician. Physicians often talk fast and in medical terms. It can be difficult trying to interpret what they are saying, as well as keeping track of all the information.

This is why it is vital that the caregiver come equipped with good listening skills, a notebook, a pen and the ability to ask questions. There is no such thing as a dumb question or a limit to how many you can ask. You are not trying to understand something simple; rather you are talking about and seeking information that is vital to your loved one's health and well-being.

Too often patients and their caregivers are intimidated by physicians and their white coats. Many assume that what the doctor has to say is flawless and is not to be questioned. When something in your gut doesn't feel right, ask questions.

Request written material from your ill loved one's doctors about the treatment being offered, possible side effects and what the success rate has been, if you want to know. They will provide you with this information.

It is very common that, whatever is said in the doctor's office, patients and their caregivers feel they will remember but forget when they arrive back home. Obtaining facts and a treatment plan can be formidable and scary. This is where that pen and paper come in handy. I recommend that you purchase a notebook and divide it into sections for medications, contacts, phone numbers and dates. Take the notebook to every doctor's appointment. Date every interaction and write down what you, your loved one and the doctor discuss. Before you leave the appointment ask when the next visit will be, as well as the best way to reach the doctor or a nurse should you have more questions, and write the information down. Both you and your loved one facing a life-threatening disease should review what is in the notebook after you get home.

You will be inundated with a multitude of things to remember. Staying organized will make both your life and your loved one's easier to handle.

I recommend that you avoid reading about diagnosis and treatment on the Internet. Information you find may not apply to your situation and may create confusion and fear. Too many people obtain inaccurate information from the Internet and react to it as though it is absolutely true about their loved ones' illnesses and must be totally applicable. If you choose to gain information on the Internet, be aware you need to discuss your findings with your loved one's medical team and do not alter or end treatments without professional medical guidance.

Topics for Reflection

1. What has been your experience with the medical team? Have you found them to be patient, open to questions and eager to explain things to you and your loved one? Or have they appeared rushed and in a hurry to move on to the next patient in the waiting room?

2. What do you perceive to be your strengths and weaknesses when interacting with the medical team on your loved one's case? If you feel timid when with them and don't feel that your needs are being met, try to visualize yourself being more assertive with them. Practicing in

the mirror at home may be helpful. I am encouraging you to speak up, because obtaining information from the medical team equals more control for you and your loved one.

3. What questions would you and your loved one like to have answered? Spend some time talking this over together and make a list to take with you and present during your next medical appointment. Otherwise it will be difficult to remember the questions once the physician is present. Do not worry about taking up the doctor's time discussing your list of concerns. It is your right and need to ask important questions and have them answered, so you don't have to second-guess any of these issues along the way.

Chapter 6

Handling Finances

There is a lot of stress related to battling a life-threatening illness and worrying about finances is very common. Even if a loved one facing a life-limiting illness receives full medical insurance coverage, many patients, their caregivers and their families face financial difficulties. Costs not covered by insurance, such as travel, hotel and meal expenses, can add up quickly and many families spend a large portion of their income on these extra fees. Additionally, the time that caregivers and their families must devote to their ill loved one may require certain family members to quit their jobs, which can have a devastating impact on the family's overall income.

Each individual's situation is different; however, there are some key points I'd like to discuss about where to turn for assistance. Keep in mind that qualifications may differ from state to state. I am providing you with an overview of the different types of disability insurance and supplemental income that may be available to your loved one. Please note that there are exceptions to every rule and some people may be able to have these benefits granted to them in a much shorter time span.

Employed Individuals

If you or your ill loved one is currently employed, contact the human resources department to determine what benefits are available for short- and long-term disability.

There are many different types of illnesses. Some require treatments that will have strong side effects and others will not. Consult your loved one's physician to get an estimate of how much work time you and/or your loved one will miss.

It is important to know whether or not a patient's illness will place him or her at risk to lose employment. You can reduce stress by discovering if your loved one's job is secure. If, on the other hand, he or she is not able to remain employed, he or she may want to apply for alternative assistance.

Medical Assistance (Medicaid)

According to Maryland's Department of Health and Mental Hygiene (DHMH), the department "provides Medical Assistance, also called Medicaid, coverage to individuals determined to be categorically eligible or medically needy. Medicaid coverage is automatically given to individuals receiving certain other public assistance, such as Supplemental Security Income (SSI), Temporary Cash Assistance (TCA), or Foster Care."[1]

Social Security Disability Insurance (SSDI)

Here is some general information about Social Security Disability Insurance, the coverage that beneficiaries can receive and the interplay with Medicare coverage, according to the Congressional Research Service:

> Social Security Disability Insurance (SSDI) beneficiaries are eligible for Medicare hospital insurance (Part A). Individuals are also eligible to purchase Medicare supplementary medical insurance (Part B) or enroll in a Medicare Advantage plan…beneficiaries will also be eligible for voluntary prescription drug benefits (Part D).
>
> Generally, SSDI beneficiaries under age 65 are eligible for Medicare coverage in the month after they received 24 months of SSDI benefits. Because of the five-month waiting period from onset of the disabling condition for disabled individuals to be

qualified to receive SSDI benefits, this results in a
total of 29 months after the onset of the disability
before an individual is eligible for Medicare benefits.
*Thus, at the beginning of the 30th month since the
onset of the qualifying disability, SSDI beneficiaries
become eligible for Medicare coverage.*[2]

The application process can be long, so you should not delay getting started. Be sure to complete the application fully, which can be done online, by phone or on paper.

The American Cancer Society (ACS)

Establishing itself as a "nationwide, community-based, voluntary health organization," the American Cancer Society (ACS) is "dedicated to eliminating cancer as a major health problem by preventing cancer, saving lives, and diminishing suffering from cancer, through research, education, advocacy and service."[3] The organization offers a wealth of material that delves into extensive details about cancer and ACS programs.

Community Help

A social worker at the hospital at which your loved one is staying or at your local health department can help put you in touch with financial assistance organizations and give advice on how to apply for hospital financial assistance. It may be worth it to explore other community-based options, such as the American Legion, Elks Club, United States Junior Chamber, Kiwanis Club, Knights of Columbus, Lions Club, Rotary Club, United Way and local churches.[4]

Personal Savings

One of the most common statements I hear from patients and their caregivers is: "I have worked hard all of my life and have put money away for retirement and to leave to others when I die. Now I have to put it toward medical expenses."

Thank goodness that there *is* a cushion. "Saving for a rainy day" is exactly that: It is a roll of the dice as to whether or not any of us will be facing unexpected illness or catastrophe.

It may be the intention of your loved one who is experiencing expensive treatment to leave money to his or her loved ones. Talk to your loved one gently about the intended recipients and discuss how those people (or you, if you are the intended) would probably much rather the ill patient use the money to keep him or herself safe and financially afloat. It may be helpful to seek assistance from a financial counselor or elder care attorney. Remember to assure your loved one that love is not defined by how much money we leave to our children or others.

Reassure the person not to feel guilty for using money that he or she saved. Rather, tell your loved one that you and he or she should be thankful he or she has it to use.

Tips for Researching and Finding Financial Aid for a Terminally Ill Loved One

- Plan ahead. Get the facts from the employer.
- Don't react but instead consider all options.
- Apply for SSDI when you or your loved one can no longer work forty-hour weeks.
- Use the Family and Medical Leave Act (FMLA), short-term and long-term disability.
- If you or your loved one leave your jobs, ask about portability of life insurance.
- Review insurance, the Consolidated Omnibus Budget Reconciliation Act (COBRA) and pensions.
- Utilize funeral assistance.
- Apply for pharmaceutical assistance from the drug manufacturer.
- Apply for Medicaid if qualified.
- Consult with legal and financial experts.

I have met many people who have felt too embarrassed to apply for financial assistance. Commonly I hear: "I have worked my whole life and never paid a bill late. I have never needed any handouts and I am not about to take any now. I am not someone who needs to be on welfare or food stamps." There is a stereotype in our society of what someone who receives financial assistance must look like.

The majority are one paycheck away from going into debt. I have watched many middle class, hardworking citizens go from being financially sound to in debt as a result of a family illness. There is a vicious cycle created from day one of diagnosis: People need to be at the hospital to receive treatment and at the same time, they need to be at work in order to earn a paycheck to pay for the treatment.

There is no shame in applying for financial aid in order to find the necessary assistance while your loved one is fighting for his or her life.

Topics for Reflection

1. Have you been in financial difficulties in the past? How were you able to overcome the problem?

2. How do you feel about possibly having to rely on financial assistance to "make ends meet"? If your attitude is negative, is there further information you can gain or people you can consult to help change the way you feel?

3. Are you confident in your knowledge about the short-term and long-term insurance benefits to which your loved one is entitled?

4. Learn all you can about the Family and Medical Leave Act (FMLA) and other state and federal programs.

Chapter 7

Taking Care of Yourself

No manual exists to explain how to be a perfect caregiver, do all your normal chores or keep up your responsibilities, such as cleaning your house, walking the dog, driving your children to activities, working at your job and being a loving spouse and parent. However, it is my experience that caregivers are so busy trying to be everything for everyone that they often forget to take care of themselves. I am sorry that your life has been completely turned upside down by someone you love being very ill and that you are hurting and worried. I know you care deeply about your loved one facing a life-limiting illness and you are probably also feeling immense loss of control and a sense of helplessness. And I know you are determined to be the best caregiver you can be. This chapter is dedicated to focusing on how to keep yourself healthy, both physically and emotionally, during this difficult journey.

The first thing airline attendants teach you before airplanes take off is what to do in the event of an emergency. They describe how the oxygen masks will fall down and your instincts will tell you to place one over your child's nose and mouth before you place one on yourself. But the airline attendants tell you this is not the correct procedure. You must first place a mask on yourself and then attend to your child. You cannot take care of others if you don't take care of yourself first. I know that you have to focus your attention on being a caretaker presently, but you will be much more effective if you follow the suggestions in this chapter.

Make Time for Yourself

Make sure to take time each day to spend time by yourself, even if it's only an hour a day. Sixty minutes out of twenty-four hours is doable. Spend time on an activity you enjoy, pursuing a hobby or relaxing in a warm bath. You deserve that and your mental health requires it.

Exercise

Move your body. Allow yourself physical motion to release stress. Your body and your mind will thank you. Exercise is a free antidepressant. If you don't already have an exercise program in place, consult your doctor and start with short walks. You can build from there as your stamina increases.

Meditation

Finding fifteen to thirty minutes to concentrate solely on your breathing is very therapeutic. If you've never tried meditation, keep an open mind. A quiet space to focus on just your breathing lowers blood pressure and can bring a sense of inner calmness to your body.

Pamper Yourself

Spend a day lounging at the spa, playing a round of golf, reading your favorite book, getting your hair done, playing cards with your friends or shopping. Whatever activity you choose is up to you. But please know that you deserve this break while being a caregiver.

Maintain Friendships

Supports are necessary during this difficult time. You are not burdening your friends with your problems; you are actually giving them a gift by allowing them to be a part of the journey. (They are feeling helpless too!) Go out to lunch, visit a museum or take a long stroll in the park with your closest friends. Having a meet-up with a friend outside of the house or hospital room can be revitalizing.

Be Selfish

Attend to your needs. Don't feel guilty for taking care of yourself, whether it's going to the doctor, getting your hair cut, visiting with a friend or simply finding time to spend alone. Think of it as a refueling requirement: Your car stops with no gas. You too will break down if you give to everyone else but yourself.

Cry

Many caregivers tell me, "I cannot cry, because I must remain strong." I disagree. Crying is not a sign of weakness but rather a sign of release. If you don't allow the fear, anxiety and sadness to come out but keep it all inside, I am concerned for your health. Crying is also the body's natural way to allow for further refueling. Think back to the last time you had a good cry. How did you feel afterwards? Many people describe it as feeling as if a weight had been lifted off their shoulders. Crying and being human go hand in hand.

Delegate

I seldom meet people who feel comfortable asking others for help. As I discussed earlier, it is much easier to give than receive. In the end, nobody is keeping tabs on how much "manpower" you put into being a caregiver and I suspect that there are many people who are calling and asking how they can help. Put them to work. Allow others to care for you and "pay it forward" in the future.

Take a Break

Find a quiet space to sit down, get comfortable and breathe deeply. Treat yourself to a glass of wine or coffee or a favorite sweet treat. Let your mind clear and enjoy sitting in quiet solitude.

Laugh and Smile

Go ahead and laugh; it is okay to smile even during this difficult time. I meet patients and families who, despite all the odds being stacked against them, are able to laugh at silly and inane things that happen during the course of difficult days and nights. Humor is a form of emotional release. Do not feel guilty for smiling, laughing or making jokes. It is therapeutic and vital to your survival.

Seek a Support Group and/or Counseling

As a caregiver for a loved one facing a life-threatening disease, you may have times when you feel alone. Remember that you are not; there are approximately sixty-five million family caregivers out there. Creating a connection with even just a few of these fellow caregivers can "foster hope and provide guidance as well as emotional and spiritual support."

The Caregiver Community Action Network (CCAN) was created as a means to "educate, provide support, and connect family caregivers to a community and each other...CCANers have all had their own family caregiving experience and now assist others to find information and support in an effort to improve their family caregiving experience and to aid in the development of important bonds with other family caregivers."[5]

There is something to be said for being among others who understand and can empathize with your situation. Support groups can be very helpful. Individual therapy provides another form of support. It will be your personal choice as to whether or not you are interested in these supports. It is my experience that seeking support from a neutral third party allows for objectivity and nonbiased feedback.

Topics for Reflection

1.　What are you doing to take care of yourself? If you aren't doing anything for yourself, begin right now. Put down this book and go for a thirty-minute walk!

2.　Who are your supports? Do you feel comfortable reaching out to them during this difficult time? Do you recognize that you cannot do this alone? If you still feel unable to ask for help, it may be beneficial to revisit some key points in this chapter.

3. Can you recognize and identify your signs of stress? For example, do you have trouble sleeping, a change in appetite, mood swings? You know yourself better than anyone; please don't ignore the signals that your body is giving to you.

4. Get assistance. This is different from reaching out for support. Get help with "hands-on stuff," like arranging the children's transportation for after-school activities, helping with meals or assisting with chores around the house.

5. Make time for yourself and other relationships.

6. Take care of your body and mind.

∽ **Chapter 8** ⌒

Caring for a Young Child with a Life-Threatening Illness

Caregivers for children who have life-limiting illnesses often feel in need of support. Allow me to express that I am sorry that your child, about whom you had so many hopes and dreams, is so very ill. For parents, this is a very difficult, emotionally-laden time. It is my hope to provide you with a sense of direction and comfort. This chapter will address the unique issues that parents face while caring for a child with a life-threatening illness and how to cope with the emotions felt within the family unit. Parents' worst nightmare is to hear that their child has a serious illness. Just as there are no parenting instructions that come with having a healthy baby, there also are no manuals for how to cope with finding out that your child is very ill. There are, though, others before you who have coped with similar difficult situations. Finding out and understanding much of what they have experienced both emotionally and physically will help to normalize the emotional roller coaster that you and your family are riding.

Parents' primary role is to love their children unconditionally and to protect them from harm's way. Think back to the first day that you became a parent: Ten fingers, ten toes and the sigh of relief when that first scream for air was heard. Once you got past the first twenty-four hours you may have had a *very* brief moment to exhale before you moved to the next set of worries. Parenting involves lots of worrying. Perhaps during a trying period in the first six months you questioned whether or not you were meant to be a parent in the first place as you stumbled around in a sleep-deprived state of mind only to emerge slowly with increased confidence as time passed and things got a little easier.

Suddenly the autopilot of parenting that you had been coasting on was stopped in its tracks when you discovered that your child had a life-limiting illness. And although each person's reaction to such news is different, it is probably safe to say that you felt a feeling of sheer panic throughout your entire body after receiving such news.

Perhaps you sat in the physician's office listening to the results of the tests and what the course of action would be going forward, but you were unable to grasp the true meaning of his words about your child. It felt like you were in a bad dream from which you wanted desperately to wake up. From that moment on, nothing would ever be the same again.

Unfortunately this is not a dream. I am going to do my best to help you through this nightmare reality. For many, the shock and disbelief that they experience after hearing such bad news can make it nearly impossible to breathe, let alone take in information. You, like so many others, probably had one very important and scary question come to mind: *Is my child going to die?* This is a question that is painful even to think about, let alone ask.

Protection Mode

Most parents go directly into protection mode and usually come up with a plan for how to "put on a happy face" in front of their child before they even leave the doctor's office. The plan usually is something like this: I must be strong and not show my child how frightened I am for him or her, because I don't want my child to panic. I cannot break down and cry in front of my child because it will scare him or her. I must remain in control and stifle my emotions so that I can forge ahead and do what I have to.

Let me share this with you: Despite your desire to camouflage your own terror and apprehension, your child can sense fear, anxiety and any change in your behavior. Your child knows, regardless of his or her age, your tempo, moods and personality better than you realize. When a shift within you takes place, your child's innate ability to sense change kicks in and your child absorbs your stress and reactions.

Despite the developmental stage of your child, I want to reinforce that your child will be deeply affected by your feelings and emotions during a crisis. It will be vital to have a balance between knowing when and how much emotion to reveal to him or her. The information in this chapter will help you gain a better understanding as well as give suggestions on taking care of yourself too. Remember, we must take care of ourselves so that we can take care of others more effectively.

Showing Emotions

We've discussed earlier that I do not believe in "shoulds" or "should nots," for example: "I should not cry in front of my child." Hearing that your child has a serious illness is overwhelming and scary. If your external expressions do not mirror your internal feelings there is sure to be a disconnection with those around you. Hiding all emotion from those whom you care about is not an effective way to deal with having a critically ill child.

Crying and showing emotion in front of your child doesn't mean that you are weak and/or not coping well. It means that you are human. Further, you are modeling for your child that is okay for him or her to show his or her emotions too. This may be your child's first experience with having to deal with complex emotions and he or she is going to be looking to you for guidance and direction. Remember, you are the life coach—lead by example!

Boundaries for Showing Emotions

It is important to understand that showing emotions in front of your child is okay and normal, but in the same regard, there are healthy boundaries that must exist in the parent-child relationship, especially when there is a crisis. Here are some guidelines for maintaining healthy emotional boundaries and avoiding unhealthy reactions:

- When showing emotions, explain to your child in age-appropriate terms what your feelings are about. For example: "Mommy is sad that you are sick and will not be able to go to school every day with your friends whom you look forward to seeing."
- Let your child know that it is okay if he or she wants to cry and show emotions. For example: "Daddy is frustrated and crying, because he wishes that he could make you all better with a snap of his fingers. Do you ever feel that way too?"
- Regain composure and provide support to your child. This shows him or her that you are in control.
- Your child should not be counseling and/or taking care of you.
- Provide reassurance that the doctors will take good care of him or her and that you will be with him or her every step of the way.
- Ask your child if he or she has any questions. Give honest answers without sugarcoating them and remember to speak in age-appropriate terms.
- Hugs can say more than words. They are free and need to be given!

Talking to Your Child

This chapter is about supporting *you*, the caregiver who has a child with a critical illness. The previous discussion on how to talk to your child when someone he or she loves has a life-threatening illness may have other good suggestions, because the themes often overlap. I feel that it is important to provide you with examples that demonstrate the difference between healthy and unhealthy exchanges with children.

First, let's look at Karen and her son, Josh, whose relationship created concern about the ways the boy's illness was being addressed. As you will see in the second rendering of the case, I endeavored to get their relationship on a more stable footing so that the boy's illness could be handled together by the parent and son to get the best possible quality of life.

The First Version of Josh's Story

Josh, a twelve-year-old, was described by his mother as "all boy." He and his friends spent their afternoons and weekends roughhousing, tossing footballs and enjoying fishing at their local creek. When asked what he wanted to be when he grew up, Josh was quick to answer, "I want to be a race car driver." He had "the need for speed," his mother Karen explained during our first meeting, several months after Josh had been diagnosed with leukemia.

The medical team had raised concerns in reference to what appeared to be an "enmeshed" relationship between mother and son. "It's as if the roles got reversed in the relationship and Josh has become a miniature adult who is taking care of his mother," Josh's physician explained to me.

I met with Josh's mother alone to get a sense of how things were going and how I could be of help. Karen came to my office looking exhausted and frail. I introduced myself, explained what my role was and asked her to describe the current and future medical plans. These questions were immediately met with tears and she requested a minute to collect herself while we sat in silence together. This reaction helped me to recognize that she was in tremendous emotional pain and I wanted to learn more about how she and her son were coping with the current events in their lives.

Karen explained that she was a single mother and that Josh was her only child. His father lived out of state and had not been present in their lives during the eight years since the couple divorced.

> **Amy:** Karen, how did you discover that something was medically wrong with Josh?
> **Karen:** He started to have frequent bloody noses and bruises all over his body, which at first I dismissed as caused by the change of seasons and the frequent tackle football games the boys play in the backyard. Several weeks later I brought him to our family doctor, because the nosebleeds were more frequent and gobs of blood flowed out.

Amy: The nosebleeds must have been scary for both of you.

Karen: Josh was just annoyed by them; I, on the other hand, was freaked out! Often during them, blood seemed to be everywhere and I *hate* the sight of blood as it is.

Amy: I can only imagine how scared you must have felt. How did you handle finding out that your son had leukemia?

Karen: It was the worst day of my life. At first, I couldn't comprehend what the doctor was saying to me and my entire body shook. I had no control over anything in that moment and I remember screaming at the physician that he had to be wrong! I sobbed for hours and tried to imagine how I was going to break the news to Josh when he returned home from school that day.

Amy: Did you call a family member or a friend to get yourself some support that day?

Karen: I couldn't. I felt paralyzed and couldn't do anything except sit in my kitchen and think about the fact that my child could die.

Amy: What was your understanding of his diagnosis and recommended treatment plan on that day?

Karen: Most of what the physician said was a complete blur, but I think she expressed that, with treatment, the odds were in Josh's favor to be cured.

Amy: Did her words ease some of your fear and anxiety?

Karen: Not on that day. I'm telling you, I was a mess and couldn't pull myself together! To be honest, I don't think I'm coping much better now than I did that day, because I am so fearful of getting bad news again. I can't imagine my son ever not being here.

Amy: How did you explain the news to your son that afternoon?

Karen: He got home from school and once I saw him I broke into tears. I could not stop crying and he, of course, was upset to see me in such a state. He handed me a box of tissues and asked me several times if someone had died. I told him that the doctor had called and explained the results of the medical tests which revealed that he had leukemia. I knew that he understood what leukemia was, because we lost a close friend of the family several years ago to this illness.

I couldn't stop crying and my son placed his arm around me, comforted me and expressed with complete calmness that we would make it through this. Thank goodness I have such a wonderful little man, because I couldn't have gotten through that day without him.

Amy: Did Josh ask you any questions about the diagnosis and what was going to happen to him going forward?

Karen: He asked if he would still be able to attend school every day and whether or not he could continue to play football with his friends. Overall, he seemed more concerned about me than for himself.

Amy: How did his reaction make you feel?

Karen: Relieved, because there was no way that I could have answered questions related to his overall prognosis, had he asked. I was thankful that he didn't ask any other questions.

Amy: So, Josh took care of you that first day? Was that typical behavior for him?

Karen: As a single parent I have had a difficult time managing the stress of working full time along with everything else. Josh often helps out around the house without my asking him to and he has always been concerned with my well-being. Sometimes I feel bad, because he wants to be "the man of the house" and take care of things that boys his age shouldn't be concerned with.

Amy: Have you ever discouraged him from owning this role?

Karen: Not as well as I could have and, to be honest, he *does* make my life much easier.

Amy: What is Josh's understanding of his illness and treatment plan at this point?

Karen: I told him that everything is going to be okay and that the doctor is going to make him better. Further, I let him know that there will be missed school days and that I was going to ask his teachers for make-up assignments in order to keep him on track.

Amy: Did he ask you any questions?

Karen: He did ask me if he had the same kind of leukemia that our family friend died of and I quickly reassured him that he didn't. I also reinforced that he would be fine.

Amy: Has Josh showed any outward emotions or changes in behavior since being diagnosed? In other words, how has he been coping with the news?

Karen: He cried once that first day but hasn't since. I don't bring anything up, because I don't want to upset him. As for his behavior, he's pretty much the same and asks me every day how I am.

This first version of Josh's story demonstrates several key issues:

- **Reversal of Roles:** From an early age Josh took on the role of taking care of his mother when she experienced stress or anxiety. He learned how to have some of his needs met through this behavior in order to compensate for his mother not being emotionally/physically available. Now that Josh is facing a life-threatening illness, he continues to attend to his mother's emotional needs versus his own.

- **Poor Boundaries:** Karen was unable to create healthy parent-child boundaries, which all children need in order to feel safe and taken care of. This was demonstrated when Josh provided comfort and reassurance to Karen that everything would be okay. Furthermore, the boundaries were blurred prior to this episode as Josh assumed the role of being the "man around the house," another attempt to take care of Karen instead of her discouraging this behavior.

- **Lack of Self-Care:** Karen had a history of anxiety and depression and was not able to reach out to professionals and/or peers to gain support and guidance. As a result, she was not able to provide comfort and support to her son, who instead internalized and felt responsible for his mother's emotions.

- **Lack of Information:** Josh was provided with very little information about current and future circumstances. This created the "monster in the closet" effect (i.e., things appear much scarier than they truly are when there is little understanding of what is going on). His only experience with leukemia was related to the family friend who passed away.

- **Lack of Support for Josh:** Children, even when they themselves are the primary patients, are often overlooked, whether it's out of a desire to protect them or to sweep the difficult issues under the rug. It happens too often and Karen, just as so many others, needed to learn how to keep her son informed and provide age-appropriate support.

Josh's Story Rewritten

Here is the same mother and son case rewritten with suggested behaviors and responses which are healthier interactions between parent and child:

> **Amy:** Karen, I want to begin by telling you how sorry I am to be meeting you under these circumstances. I would be lying to you if I said that I know how you are feeling. What I can connect with is the extreme loss of control that you are probably feeling.
>
> **Karen:** I am definitely feeling that, along with being overwhelmed and scared. I am hoping that these meetings will provide my son and me some much-needed support.
>
> **Amy:** That is my hope too and since this is our first time meeting, is it okay if I ask you some questions in order to get to know you better?
>
> **Karen:** Yes, that would be fine.
>
> **Amy:** Can you help me understand what is being interrupted in your lives right now?
>
> **Karen:** I am a single parent and we depend on my income and health insurance. I have not been able to work since Josh was diagnosed and if it weren't for the fact that my boss has been supportive, I probably would have lost my job by now. He has assured me that my position is being held, but once I use all my sick and vacation days, I don't know what will happen to my income. My coworkers have started a fund and have also donated over a month's worth of their sick days to me. These gestures amaze me and I don't know how I will ever be able to thank them enough for what they are doing to help me.
>
> **Amy:** I am glad to hear that people are reaching out to give you support. I hope that some of your stress is being reduced so that you can place more attention

on your son. Your coworkers are helping you because they care and I would bet on the fact that they are not keeping tabs or wanting anything in return. There will come a time in your future when you will have an opportunity to pay it forward to someone else in need. Right now, focus on taking care of yourself and your son.

Karen: I don't think that I could focus on anything else even if I wanted to. I am so scared about my son's health right now that everything else has taken a backseat. I feel like an emotional wreck.

Amy: Karen, what you're saying is completely normal and I am not going to let you do this alone. How did you discover that Josh was sick and what has your physician explained to you in reference to what the medical plan will be going forward?

Karen: Josh is your typical boy. He likes to play football with his friends and it's not abnormal for him to be bruised from their tackling and roughhousing. A few weeks ago I noticed bruises all over his body and he was getting bloody noses three to four times a day. At first I attributed the nosebleeds to the change in seasons, but when they became more severe I made an appointment with our primary care physician.

Amy: That must have been scary for you both.

Karen: I don't think that it ever occurred to me or to Josh that anything serious was going on. I assumed that his doctor would simply examine him, write some prescriptions for his allergies and send us on our way. I was not prepared for the phone call that I received stating that I needed to make an appointment as soon as possible to discuss the blood work results.

Amy: Did Josh go to the appointment with you?

Karen: No, the doctor asked that I come alone, which really scared me. And since I didn't know what he was going to tell me, I decided not to mention the meeting to Josh ahead of time. I'm glad that I didn't bring him, because I was an emotional wreck after hearing that he has leukemia.

Amy: What do you mean by "emotional wreck," Karen?

Karen: The physician was explaining that Josh had leukemia and before he could finish his sentence I broke down. I tried to collect myself, but my hands were shaking and the tears wouldn't stop flowing. I was a mess.

Amy: Actually, your reaction sounds right on target to me and I would have been concerned if you had told me that you were fine.

Karen: That's relieving, because I felt so embarrassed in the doctor's office that day. He was wonderful and took over an hour of his time to explain everything, answer all of my questions and, most importantly, let me know that the odds are in Josh's favor to achieve remission.

Amy: I am glad that the physician was able to provide you with some comfort and it sounds like he was able to give you a strong message of hope. How did you explain everything to Josh?

Karen: I went home and sat at the kitchen table for hours while my mind raced between good and bad thoughts. I couldn't help but think about the possibility of losing my son to leukemia. I allowed myself to cry until I couldn't cry any longer and I then collected

myself prior to Josh arriving home from school. I
knew that I had to control some of my emotions in
order to be strong.

Josh knew the minute that he walked in the door
that something was wrong due to my swollen, red
eyes. We sat down and I explained to him that the test
results revealed that he has leukemia. I shared that
the doctor seemed confident that the medication and
treatment will be able to "kick the leukemia's butt"
and hopefully cure him.

Josh's eyes opened wide and he had a look of panic
on his face. He said to me, "Mom, didn't Mr. Dave
have leukemia? The medication didn't work for him.
Am I going to die too?"

My heart sank with that question and I began to
cry again. I told him, "Josh, that is such a good question and I'm glad that you thought to ask it. Mr. Dave
had a different type of leukemia. We are going to
one of the best doctors and right now there is every
reason to believe that you are going to survive this.
I know that you don't like to cry, but it's okay if you
want to, because this is probably hard to handle."

Josh asked me many questions at that point. He
wanted to know if he would have to miss school,
whether or not he could continue to play with his
friends, how long everything would take, whether or
not there would be many needles and how would I be
able to go to work every day.

I knew that Josh was feeling as much loss of
control as I was feeling so I didn't brush off any of
his questions. This was the hardest conversation that
I have ever had with my child and, although I felt as

though I was falling apart inside, I tried to appear to be in control and calm on the outside.

Amy: I applaud your ability to be "present" for your son, because I know how difficult that must have been. I also want to reinforce one very important thing that you did an excellent job at: You gave him honest answers and knew how to manage his questions. Further, you modeled for him that it was okay for him to show his emotions and you had enough insight not to "lose it" completely in front of him. I meet many parents who wouldn't have been able to handle things the way you did that day. You took care of your son in that moment despite your own despair. *Much* easier said than done, Karen.

Karen: Your words are helpful, because I am filled with insecurities right now about how to handle all of this. I don't always know what the right thing to say is, especially when he asks tough questions. I want to promise him that everything is going to be fine, that he will be cured and go on to live a long and happy life, but I know that there are no guarantees right now.

Amy: Let me assure you that most parents feel insecure with how to answer the tough questions. You are trying to protect your son from emotional pain, which I refer to as the "high wire performance," because it is a balancing act that parents struggle with: hope versus despair. In order to make it across the high wire without falling, small, thoughtful steps must be taken, ever so gently. Too much weight on either side (hope or despair) can cause an abrupt fall, so the goal is to balance the weight evenly throughout. This takes a lot of practice and falls *will* occur.

The important step is to get back up, recognize where the imbalances took place and shift the weight again. Nobody gets across the wire without falling several times. This is a series of steps that you both will take together and your job is to be "present" for his falls and to help him climb back up.

Karen: Your words are relieving and I think that I've done a fairly good job of being present. Each day I try to check in with him, ask how he is feeling and continue to keep the door open for questions. He seldom talks about his illness, though, and that concerns me.

Amy: I think that it is wonderful that you have a daily check-in and please continue with that. I would also like to suggest that you model for him how to talk about his feelings. As his parent, you play the role of life coach. Coaches lead by example. Share with him how you are feeling, but make sure that it's age-appropriate and that you are not seeking comfort from him.

In this case, the interactions between Karen and her son Josh were healthy and appropriate. She provided a safe place for Josh to ask questions and show his emotions while also presenting the information and honest answers he needed.

Here are some additional examples of better parent-child interactions that allow both parent and child to express emotions:

- "I felt happy today hearing the doctor say that things are going well. I sure hope that it stays that way. Sometimes I get worried that the treatments may make you feel tired or not well. I would imagine that you miss being able to attend school and seeing your friends every day. I know that I would feel that way if it were me."

- "I am so proud of how you are handling all of this. I don't know about you, but sometimes I just feel like punching my pillow out of frustration when certain things happen in life that I can't control. I might look really silly doing it, but I tend to feel a little better afterwards. Do you ever feel that way?"
- "I am so proud of how you are handling all of this. I don't know about you, but it has been really helping me to talk with other people about all of the changes in our lives. I was provided with information about a place that has support groups for kids and I am wondering if you would like to go. It may be helpful to interact with others who are going through many of the same things that you are. I've also been told that the kids get to do many fun things together. I am not going to make you go; it's your choice. Perhaps you'd like to attend once to check it out. If you don't like it, you don't have to go back."

Remember that it is okay and even healthy to cry in front of your child, because it is a form of modeling and will give your child permission to show emotion without feeling embarrassed.

Points to Remember

- You and your child need to know that having fun is not only still possible, but also necessary!
- Children need to feel a sense of being in control too. (e.g., "You can attend the support group if you want. I am not going to force you to go.") Giving choices allows them to feel more in control.
- Children learn coping skills from their parents. Model for your child that it is normal to experience a range of emotions (sadness, anger, fear, loneliness).
- Although you play a pivotal role in your child's life, it's important that you provide him or her with space to explore additional avenues of support (e.g., support groups, therapy, friends).

- Teach your child that there are many different ways that he or she can express his or her feelings (e.g., writing in a journal, creating artwork or blogging, depending on age).
- Encourage your child to get dirty! Allow me to explain: My daughter attended a day care center when she was a toddler and on one particular afternoon I overheard an upset parent complaining to the director, because her child's clothes were dirty. I thought this an odd complaint, because her son was only three years old and had spent the day running around and having fun. The upset parent mandated that the staff not allow him ever to get dirty, because it might ruin his clothes. My daughter was covered with dirt, smiling and playing with the other children. What a wonderful sight! In my opinion, she was fully experiencing her childhood. That was *her* rite of passage before having to learn some of life's tougher lessons in the years to follow. Years later I overheard my daughter telling a friend, "My mother always said that the sign of a good day is to come home dirty."
- Know when to "step back" in order to give your child the space needed to experience life in the moment, even while he or she is sick.

Your child will always need your guidance and support—the key is to allow for some dirty clothes as well.

Who is Taking Care of You?

Recent statistics indicate that nearly half of marriages end in divorce and that it has also become more socially acceptable to be a single parent. Those facts indicate that when your child is diagnosed with a life-threatening illness you could be married, divorced, in an alternative relationship, widowed or single. Each scenario brings a vast difference in relation to supports for a caregiver. No matter what situation applies to you, every family unit experiences suffering. The support and examples I provide can be applied to anyone who has a sick child.

Having a child diagnosed with a life-limiting illness is life-changing. The range of emotions that you are feeling is normal and expected:

- **Shock**: The inability to comprehend that your child has a life-limiting illness. People often describe the feeling of shock as an out-of-body experience. They are present in the moment physically but not mentally.
- **Denial:** Individuals are not able to accept that something has happened at that point in time. (e.g., "There must be some mistake. My child can't be sick.")
- **Anger:** It is common to feel angry at the world. People are often angry at whatever they cannot control. Many parents question, "Why my child? What did we do to deserve this?"
- **Depression:** Overwhelming feelings of despair and hopelessness. Some parents are emotionally numb upon first hearing the diagnosis. They do not feel like getting out of bed each day, let alone managing all the medical care that the critically ill child will require. This can last for a long period of time.
- **Anxiety:** One day, life can be calm and manageable. The next, it can be complete chaos. Anxiety is often felt when there is little direction for how to solve a problem. A life-limiting illness easily creates a sense of urgency and chaos without advance notice or direction. Parents often feel a constant sense of panic.
- **Loss of Control:** Everything changes in areas such as schedules, home life, work and the emotions that accompany these changes. Parents may feel they can't handle being unable to manage everything.

Hearing that your child is sick is a traumatic event and it is common to feel many of these emotions. They will often shift and change in intensity based on where you and your child are in the journey. You are human and will experience highs and lows that your internal system is trying to regulate, but it cannot adjust without support.

Effects on Marriage

Every marriage is different but over the years I have witnessed common themes that can occur between partners when they face difficult times, especially when a child is critically ill.

- The relationship strengthens.
- The relationship falls apart.
- The relationship becomes distanced, with both individuals existing in the same house but living separate lives.

You and your spouse entered marriage full of hopes and dreams for a future which could not have predicted the events that you are facing now. Although you are united in marriage, you are two separate people who have been shaped by different pasts. Often, it is not until a crisis occurs that each person's ability or lack of ability to cope under stress becomes visible. This is very normal and is nobody's fault, but if the serious illness of your child is creating a separation within the marriage, it is vital that both partners seek neutral, outside support in hopes of being able to reconnect.

Roles Change

When a child becomes very sick, roles often change in order to support the needs of the situation. Remember, the entire family is affected and daily schedules, routines and normal expectations are now disorganized, chaotic and out of sync. Here are some common changes parents with a critically ill child experience:

- One parent must stay home to provide the care and support the child needs (given that, in many households, both adults work).
- One parent must be present at work, become the sole provider and probably the carrier of the household's health insurance.
- One parent must be able to provide attention and care to the other children in the house.

- One parent may be emotionally fragile while the other is feeling pressured to remain strong.
- Both parents may be falling apart, feeling numb and unable to attend to anything other than their child's needs.

These changes in roles can generate a host of feelings that were not otherwise present within the relationship. Resentment and anger are common emotions felt as the changes continue over time. One parent may feel that he or she is doing more than the other or more commonly express that one role may be more important than the other. For example:

- "I am home all day and haven't even had time to take a shower. You get to leave the house and catch your breath. The least that you can do is come home after work and take over for me."
- "My day at the office was insane and I can't seem to make any progress. You just don't get it. I am exhausted too when I come home and whatever I do isn't enough for you."

Most relationships struggle due to the change in roles, exhaustion, stress and the ever-changing emotions that are present. Sadly, this can create feelings of isolation and lack of needed support for both partners.

There *is* hope! Underneath the complex layers of these new issues around your critically ill child is the foundation of love which brought you and your partner together in the first place. Remember, neither of you can dictate or control how your feelings and emotions will be experienced, but you can be in control of how you go forward by seeking support conducive to your present situation:

- **Couples Counseling:** Can provide a neutral, safe place to discuss and receive guidance about issues at hand. You are both in crisis mode and having a third party intervene can be very helpful.
- **Support Groups:** Although your situation is unique, the other members who attend these groups have experienced many of

the same feelings and emotions and are capable of providing support to you that others can't.

- **Individual Therapy:** A safe environment where you can "verbally throw up." When used correctly, a good therapist can be life changing.
- **Close Friends:** Make time to talk with your closest friends, whether it's on the phone or meeting over lunch.
- **Family Members:** Many families are built around a lifetime of love and support. If you come from a close family and/or have someone within it who has helped you in times of crisis, ask for help.

It is very important that you pursue a support system, no matter which option is the right fit for you and your needs. Over time it is my hope that you and your spouse are able to find "common ground," composed of the love and support that you both need from each other.

Relationships are hard work to maintain under the best of circumstances. Try to remember that you are both scared and filled with many complex feelings that will hopefully strengthen the unity that you have, now and in the future.

Handling Guilt

The range of emotions that you feel will most likely be moving back and forth and in-between. At any given time, you may feel that you are doing okay one minute and ready to fall apart the next. This is normal and I would be concerned if you weren't experiencing these emotions. One of the common feelings that goes hand-in-hand with this type of situation is guilt.

Guilt is such a strong emotion and it can play havoc on parents who have a critically ill child. Parents often blame themselves and feel that they must have done something wrong to make their child sick.

- "I should have taken him to the doctor sooner."
- "This is my punishment for doing something wrong."
- "I didn't protect my child well enough."

You have done *nothing* wrong! You do not possess the power and control to have caused your child to become sick. There is a huge difference between feelings of sadness that your child is sick versus feelings of guilt, because you think that you "made your child sick." There is *nothing* that you could have done differently that would have prevented the current situation.

Let's acknowledge your pain and feelings of immense loss of control. If you haven't cried lately to release some of the pain and you feel you really want to let it out in this way, I encourage you to find some time and space to do so. I know that you are scared and you spend sleepless nights worried and terrified about your child's future. You are experiencing the loss of control I previously discussed. Now let me help you understand what you *do* have in your control:

Hope

In the cases of several life-threatening illnesses, research and professionals have made many discoveries and advances. Children with diseases which in the past could not be cured are now able to achieve full remissions and/or are living much longer lives.

Self-Care

Remember what we've shared earlier in this book. You cannot take care of others if you do not take care of yourself. Your child needs you. He or she needs a parent with resilience and strength, not a parent who is exhausted and depleted.

It is important to take thirty to sixty minutes a day for you. From years of experience coaching seriously ill patients and their families, I want you to know that despite your child being very ill, you *can and should* make time for yourself. Making time for yourself is especially important in this emotionally taxing time. Without self-care, you are putting yourself on a path to burnout. Additionally, your child will need a break from you (despite his or her age); time alone is necessary for everyone. When friends, family and neighbors ask what they can do to help, discuss with them dates and times they can give you short breaks and mark the dates on your calendar in order to get some "you time." There are many ways to spend these breaks, such as taking a hot bath or going for a run. Just make sure that the time is focused on you and your needs only.

Advocate

You have more control than you realize over what will or will not happen to your child. Make your questions, concerns and wishes heard during medical appointments. Ask as many questions as you want and do *not* worry about the physician's and medical team's feelings. They treat hundreds of ill children each year, but this is *your* child and having a strong sense of direction is vital to your regaining some control in your life. Knowledge is power. If you understand the current and future treatment plans, then you will be better prepared to talk to your child and answer questions.

Feelings and Emotions

Every person copes differently. Some feel paralyzed with sadness and can't get out of bed for days at a time. Others launch into action mode and appear not to take a break. Then there are those who just try to trudge through the days while experiencing constant feelings of sadness, anger, anxiety, etc. But there comes a point when you need to shift your mindset and attempt to forge ahead.

After years of meeting many diverse individuals who are patients with life-threatening illnesses or their caregivers, I am still amazed at the inner strength and human spirit that people have during times of crisis. You have control over positive versus negative thinking. Though low moments will still exist, your child and family need you to dig deep within and find an inner strength that you may never have known you possessed. I promise you have it within you.

Know When to Get Help

You are not failing or letting anyone down if you are feeling numb, stuck and in need of assistance. Stressful events such as having a critically ill child can release an underlying or present mental health concern with which you may need help. The key is to know when to seek help.

Depression and anxiety are the two most common issues with which I help caregivers cope and both can be treated with the proper supports and/or medications. Some people do not want to take medications and may elect counseling. However, if you are still experiencing depression and anxiety and decide to take medication, one of two things can happen: It may take the edge off and make what feels unbearable more tolerable or it may do nothing. Taking medication during such a stressful time does not mean that you are weak. Be aware, though, that there is no medication that will take away the emotional pain completely.

Handling Reactions from Others

If you haven't already experienced the vastly different reactions that you will hear from those around you when you tell them your loved one has a life-threatening or terminal illness, understand that their comments are said with good intentions even though they may leave a feeling of rage within you. Here are some real examples of what others may say to a parent of a critically ill child:

- "I am so sorry that your child is sick. I just don't know what I would do if it was my daughter."
- "I can't even imagine what you must be going through."
- "You are being so strong. How are you holding it together?"
- "'Everything is going to be okay. I know how you feel."
- "One of my friend's daughters had leukemia. She was treated at the same hospital. Sorry to say that she didn't make it. Oh, but your son will be fine, I am sure."
- "I was sorry to hear about your son. We are here if you need anything. Did I tell you that our son got straight As this semester and made the varsity basketball team?"

I do not think that such comments are meant to be hurtful or insensitive, but they often leave a deep emotional reaction in the caregiver who is struggling with his or her own emotional upheaval at the time.

Why Do People Say Such Things?

People who know and care about you also are "walking on eggshells" and have difficulty finding the right words to communicate their compassion and feelings about your loved one's crisis. People are scared and insecure, so they stumble and grasp at their words. Try to think back to what you would have said to a friend in crisis prior to your current situation. Would the words have come out differently back then?

As much as you might like to scream at the top of your lungs, use your control to abstain. Your energy is needed elsewhere. No one will ever be able to understand the exact situation you are experiencing.

Remember that the advice and information in this book is intended for caregivers, who are the silent heroes who walk alongside someone who has a life-limiting illness. I want to let you know you are *not* alone on this difficult journey. The focus of this book is on helping you give unconditional love and support, which are the main components to being an effective caregiver as well as caring for yourself. My intention is to aid you in progressing through the steps of caring for a child with a life-threatening illness.

Topics for Reflection

1. Have you been able to cry and show emotion in front of your child in the past? That doesn't mean you are weak. You are modeling for your child that is okay for him or her to show his or her emotions too. Lead by example.

2. Are you truly willing to give your child the space to explore additional avenues of support, to "get dirty," to experience life in the moment?

3. Are you able to have an open dialogue with your child and family regarding current events? If not, I encourage you to "push" yourself forward on this topic, because communication makes situations more bearable for everyone.

4. If you have experienced a situation in the past that created a high level of stress, how did you manage that? What was most helpful?

5. Are you able to reach out to others to get support? If not, what is holding you back?

ᕽ Chapter 9 ᕽ

Caring for an Adult Child with a Life-Threatening Illness

No matter how old children are, parents' innate need to protect their children from pain and discomfort continues throughout their lifetimes. Knowing how to become a caregiver for your adult child can be conflicting, as your adult child attempts to hold onto every ounce of independence he or she has achieved prior to becoming ill. Serious illness affects everyone in the family and your relationship with your adult child could vary, depending on how close you are and whether there are others in your child's life.

While you may be ready to drop everything to help, your adult child may be slowing or denying your efforts. Remember, being diagnosed with a life-limiting illness leads to feelings of immense loss of control.

Let's discuss some possible reasons why your loved one may hesitate to talk with you and/or involve you in the process. Some young adults don't want to share their troubles, because they feel guilty about worrying their parents. Furthermore, your adult child may have other supports available to him or her such as a partner, spouse and/or close friends who are being utilized as well.

Your critically ill adult child may experience some of these difficult problems and feelings:

- Emotional and physical changes/limitations
- Increased anxiety

- Lowered or negative self-image and body image
- Sexual and reproductive issues
- Uncomfortable side effects from treatments/medications
- Recurrence of symptoms

These issues can be difficult to sort through and your adult child may not feel comfortable talking to you about personal issues. Further, he or she may perceive you as being overprotective or trying to take charge if you push him or her to keep you involved every step of the way. Try to respect your child's needs and wishes. Remind him or her that you are available if he or she needs assistance with anything or just someone to talk with, but be sure to let him or her know that he or she is not obligated to share everything with you. It is my hope that your loved one will know that your actions are due to the love that you have for him or her; in the meantime, don't be put off by his or her actions.

Practical Assistance

If your adult child is open to receiving your help, here are some practical things that you can do:

- Accompany him or her to doctor and hospital visits.
- Gather information, do research and take notes at medical appointments.
- Help your loved one make sense of the medical bills and insurance statements.
- Organize finances and medical records.
- Help with household chores.
- Update family and friends (provided that he or she wants to share the latest news about how things are progressing).
- Keep an open line of communication with your adult child. Remind him or her that asking for help doesn't mean that he or she has lost his or her independence, but that it is fulfilling practical and financial needs.

Your loved one with a life-threatening illness could experience a range of emotions such as loneliness, depression, anxiety, etc. Here are some examples of issues with which your adult child may struggle:

- Lack of independence
- Isolation from friends and social activities
- Dissolution of friendships and/or relationships due to the illness
- Loss of employment or having to leave college
- Strained marriage
- Inability to care for children
- Inability to contribute to family income
- Insecurities about physical appearance due to the side effects of treatments

Living Arrangements

Many young adults who become ill prefer not to move back home with their parents after they've established a life of independence, but there are times when this is the only practical answer to getting needed physical support when someone is critically ill. Your loved one may be having a difficult time with this transition and feel like he or she is giving up his or her "life." I encourage you bring these two points to your adult child's attention:

1. Your adult child is taking control of his or her life by attending to his or her emotional, practical and financial needs.
2. Your adult child is giving his or her family a gift by allowing them to assist in his or her care.

You may want to consider moving in with your adult child for a brief time, which would allow your child to feel more in control. Everyone's circumstances are different and what may fit the needs of one family may not fit the needs of another. Although you may still think of your adult child as being someone who depends on you, try to be mindful of asking him or her what his or her wishes are. Your child is an adult and needs to be treated as such.

Finding Balance Between Your Child's Spouse and You

It could be very difficult for your adult child to know how to accept your help if he or she is married. Your child will most likely feel torn between his or her spouse and you and may experience feelings of guilt if he or she doesn't know how to balance the two. There is a difference between the support that we receive from our families and that of our life partner. One is not better than the other—they are just different and they meet separate needs. These issues are normal between families. Try not to take your ill adult child's actions personally while under the current stressors. If you notice that your adult child is feeling torn between you and his or her spouse, you may wish to bring it up as a topic for which you can provide support.

Medical Appointments and Hospitalizations

Remember when your child was young and there were doctor appointments for the flu, yearly checkups, dental cleanings and many other visits? You needed to answer all of the questions pertaining to your child for the doctor. When children are young, parents speak for their children if they don't have the ability or knowledge to give information about themselves. Eventually children turn into adults who have voices of their own. Old habits are hard to break and being in a hospital or at medical appointments tends to reignite the parental urge to become the spokesperson for an adult child. Many parents don't even realize that they are playing this old role.

The next time that you accompany your loved one to an appointment or visit him or her while he or she is in the hospital, remember that while your input is important and worthwhile, you must let your adult child speak for him or herself and ask his or her desired questions before you give your opinion. I recommend that you ask your child prior to medical appointments if he or she minds you voicing your feedback and/or questions. Remember, you want to help your adult child maintain a sense of control throughout this process. His or her voice, independent of yours, is the best way to do this.

Family Feuds

Given that your adult child has been living on his or her own, there could be things that you haven't approved of (e.g., other people in his life) or perhaps things that you don't know about. I have witnessed families fall apart when other people in the patient's life interact with the patient's parents. There have been behavioral contracts made or visiting hours taken away due to one party not getting along with the other party.

No family is exempt from having its share of issues. Get in touch with your issues now and it may help you and your family with the problems and unforeseen conflicts. The focus needs to be on the patient and not the years of family dynamics that continue to exist. It is important in the current crisis to put these disagreements and conflicts aside.

Support for Your Adult Child

Many adult children will not want to be told what to do and may in fact get upset at parents' suggestions for locating outside support. A better way of broaching this topic is to ask your child if he or she would be interested in finding some external support and if so, ask if it would be helpful if you located some groups or if your child would prefer to do this on his or her own. Here is some helpful information about locating support for your adult child facing a life-limiting disease:

- The supports for young adults are similar to those for adults. Some counties have support groups that specialize in providing support to young adults, but most are geared toward adults in general.
- Subsets of support groups are geared toward particular illnesses (e.g., leukemia and lymphoma, breast cancer, prostate cancer, Parkinson's disease, heart diseases, ALS) and many can be located by contacting the American Cancer Society or other national associations or by calling a hospital that is close to where you live.
- Some camps offer support to young adults and can be contacted by calling national groups which you can locate by doing a search on the Internet.

- Individual therapy can be an avenue to receive support and work through personal issues.
- Life-threatening illnesses affect the entire family. This may be an appropriate time to consider family therapy to help sort through past and present issues in order to move forward in unity.

Kim's Story

Kim, a twenty-four-year-old woman, was diagnosed with leukemia two days prior to my meeting her during her first hospitalization. She had graduated from college with a degree in political science and landed her first job a year before getting sick. Her parents were divorced and both had remarried many years ago. Between the two sets of parents she had five siblings and she described her family as being close but not without its own set of dysfunctions. She went onto explain to me that her biological parents did not get along and that there had been years of stress, because the children felt caught in the middle.

Kim was supporting herself and lived with two roommates, several hours away from where her family resided. She was not in a romantic relationship and enjoyed hanging out with her friends and going to clubs on the weekends.

> **Amy**: What is your understanding of your diagnosis and the plan going forward?
>
> **Kim**: I have leukemia and it is my understanding that I am to begin treatment tomorrow. The doctors told me that if I had to get cancer, this is one of the easiest ones to treat, but I don't know if I should trust that.
>
> **Amy**: Do you know anyone who has had cancer?
>
> **Kim**: My aunt had breast cancer and she passed away several years ago. She thought that she could beat it, but wasn't able to. So, I'm not very trusting of medicine and doctors. But I have no other choice other than to hope that they are right.

Amy: That must have been a painful time in your life and I imagine that this current news must be stirring up all of those feelings. There are no two identical cancers and each person's body responds to treatment differently. I know it will be hard, but try not to compare yourself to your aunt's situation, because yours is completely different. I think that there's every reason to be hopeful right now that things will go well. How did you and your family cope with that time period?

Kim: We all kind of fell apart for a few months. My aunt was my mother's sister and they were very close. My mother took it the hardest and she spent many days crying and taking naps. I understood her way of coping and we as a family supported her. My stepfather is a great guy and he took up the slack regarding the needs of the house and helping us.

Amy: It sounds like your mother experienced a significant depression after your aunt passed away. It must have been hard for you to see her in pain and not know what to do to make it better.

Kim: Yes, it was very hard, but I was away at college and distracted by the events that surrounded me. I kept in regular touch with my mother and in time she worked through it.

Amy: What is your disease interrupting in your life? Do you work or are you married or have children?

Kim: I am employed at a local firm that reviews policies for local companies and I love it there. Everyone is very nice and we go out for happy hour once a month. I am single, have never been married and don't have any children. I live with two girlfriends with whom I went to college and we all get along really well. They both work full time and we enjoy hanging out together.

Amy: It sounds like you have successfully entered the adult world and are doing well. How are you handling this current situation?

Kim: (*beginning to cry*) I am really scared. What if the treatment doesn't work?

Amy: Kim, your anxious feelings are normal; in fact, I would be concerned if I didn't hear that you are scared. This *is* scary and I would imagine that you are feeling an immense loss of control right now. You have been yanked right out of your life. I wish that I could tell you that everything is going to be okay, but I don't know that. Instead, I am going to make sure that you don't do this alone.

Kim: I feel a bit better just being able to talk to you and have a good cry. My mother is coming here later today.

Amy: How is your family handling this news?

Kim: They are scared too. My parents cried while we were talking on the phone last night and I couldn't hold it together hearing them. I know that this is really hard for my mother and I am afraid that she won't be able to handle all of this in addition to my aunt's death.

Amy: I haven't met your mother yet, but she may be stronger than you think. Again, you are a separate person from your aunt and your mother has a completely different relationship with you.

Kim: Yeah, I understand. I just feel bad for putting her through this.

Amy: Please understand, *you are not putting her through this*. You did not make this happen and you have nothing to feel guilty about. This is bad luck and it is not happening for any reason other than the fact that cancer doesn't discriminate.

Kim: Thank you. I needed to hear that today.

Amy: Let's talk about some realistic needs that you will probably have while you are going through treatment. Following this admission, you will need to come back and forth to the outpatient center two to three times per week to have labs drawn and you will need blood products about once a week. The medical team doesn't always prepare patients for these needs until it is time for discharge, so I wanted to get you thinking about who will be your supports during this crucial time. You also will need a twenty-four-hour caregiver in case you have any reaction to the medications. The hospital administration will not discharge you unless you can provide them with who these people will be.

Kim: I was hoping that I could return to my apartment and work at least part time, but after listening to you none of that appears to be possible. I don't have anyone who can take me back and forth or stay with me twenty-four/seven, because my roommates work.

Amy: What about your family? Do your mother and father work full time?

Kim: I am not asking them to be my caretakers. That would mean that I would have to move back home. I do *not* want to do that!

Amy: Kim, I understand that this would not be your first choice, but hear me out. I know that you are used to your independence and doing things your way on your time. If I were you, the last thing that I'd want to do is to move back home. But this may be your only option if you are to give yourself the best odds to beat this disease. If you move back home it will not be forever. The hope is to get back into your

life as you knew it as soon as possible. Your parents
love you and are feeling a loss of control too. You are
giving them a gift by allowing them to help you and
to be involved. If it would make you feel better, I can
ask them to come for a family meeting and we can
all discuss what will work best for you while you are
staying at home.

Kim: I understand what you are saying and I will
discuss my aftercare needs with my mother this afternoon and get her input. It *would* be very helpful if we
have a family meeting before I go home to make sure
that they respect my privacy, among other things.

Amy: I know that all of this is hard to adjust to and
everything must feel like it's happening very fast. Let's
try to take things one hour at a time right now versus
months ahead. I will be here every step of the way.

I took time to communicate with Kim so she clearly understood her
diagnosis and what the treatment plan was to be. I worked to normalize
her feelings and provide emotional support while reassuring Kim that she
would not make the journey alone. I helped Kim to understand why she
would need the support of her family and I provided short-term goals
(e.g., staying with her parents for a limited time versus moving back in
for good).

Kim and her family worked out temporary living arrangements and
everyone pitched in to provide the support that she needed. There were
many family meetings to "tweak" the plan every few weeks, but together
they made it work for everyone. Eventually Kim's doctors pronounced
Kim as being in full remission and she went back to living on her own and
thriving at her job.

Kim's case demonstrates the struggles that many young adults experience when they first learn that they have life-limiting illnesses. Understandably, they are not prepared for the bad news that that they receive

or the major changes in their lives. Adult children continue to need their parents' unconditional love but they need to make their own decisions and have their plans heard.

Topics for Reflection

1. Were you able to connect with the issues brought up in this chapter in reference to your relationship with your adult child? If so, are there areas that you'd like to change? How?

2. What conversations would you want to have with your adult child right now if he or she was sitting in your presence?

3. What would you like your adult child to be sharing differently with you? Do you now feel capable of asking him or her to share?

4. Who is giving you support during this difficult time? Who can you contact if you need further support?

5. Do you think that you have been successful in giving your adult child control during this time period? How will you begin or continue to accomplish and/or improve this?

Chapter 10

Caring for a Spouse with a Life-Threatening Illness

Weddings are days meant for celebration and are filled with hopes and dreams for a happy and healthy future. Promising to love forever, for richer or poorer, for better or worse seems so natural, but it isn't until one of the spouses is diagnosed with a life-threatening illness that what it means to support someone "for better or for worse" becomes a reality. The difficult journey going forward is built upon the foundation of love that brought you and your partner together in the first place. Whether you are a young, middle-aged or older couple, you will both be tested in ways which will define and redefine new layers of your union.

Moments That Make History

Each generation connects with pivotal moments in history. For example, some remember the assassination of President Kennedy as if it were yesterday. They can describe exactly where they were, what they were doing and many other details that ordinarily are forgotten as time passes. Others have similar memories of the Space Shuttle *Challenger* disaster or can still see vivid images from September 11, 2001. When such a traumatic event happens during your lifetime, it will never be forgotten.

Learning your spouse has a life-limiting illness is a personal historical moment that will endure from that day forward. Although everything following that moment may be blurred, the information provided that day will probably be replayed over and over again in your mind. The physician may have only used twenty to thirty minutes to explain the diagnosis, but you will carry memories of the day with you for a lifetime.

Handling your spouse's life-threatening illness requires medical, personal and other help. Prior chapters have discussed what the common emotional reactions are when you find out that your loved one is terminally ill. Now let's focus on unique issues that you may be experiencing.

Roles Change

Every couple designs their relationship around individual roles such as who cleans the house, pays the bills, cuts the grass, cares for the children and supports the family financially. Perhaps taking on additional tasks after your spouse is diagnosed with a life-threatening disease doesn't appear to be difficult at first, but when combined with the varied emotions that you are trying to handle, each task can feel monumental. When your loved one became terminally ill, the spousal roles changed and, as mentioned before, this can create a host of feelings for you, the caregiver. In the beginning, sheer adrenaline may allow caregivers to feel they can take on both spousal roles, but eventually, exhaustion will take effect. If at any time during the process you feel you have lost perspective on taking care of yourself, refer to the guidelines in chapter eight and throughout this book. Remember, you cannot care for your loved one effectively without also taking care of yourself.

Steve's Story

Steve was forty-five years old and had been married to Annie for fourteen years. Together they had two preteens. Steve was a devoted church member and owned his own company. He was in good health and exercised regularly but began to notice that he was losing weight and waking up each night drenched. A visit to his primary physician revealed that his white blood count level was abnormal and his physician referred Steve to a local oncologist for further evaluation. The oncologist's preliminary tests revealed that Steve had pancreatic cancer and he was told to come to the hospital immediately to start treatment.

I met with Steve and his wife during his first of many hospitalizations and provided emotional support from that point forward. The issues that he and his wife struggled with are very common.

> **Amy:** I wanted to meet with you both today to catch up on how things have been going at home prior to this hospitalization.
>
> **Steve:** (*tearful*) Things have not been going well. These treatments have been taking such a toll on me and all that I've been able to do is sleep most of the days. I try to help around the house as much as I can, but my energy level seems to last for thirty minutes and then I am exhausted.
>
> Everything has been falling on Annie and I feel like such a burden. I received news from the doctor this morning that my cancer is not responding to the chemotherapy and he wants to add radiation to the treatment plan. I am so discouraged and of no use to my family. Perhaps it is time to stop everything and be done with all of this.
>
> **Annie:** Steve, how can you say such things? You are *not* a burden and you have valid reasons for not being able to perform your everyday tasks. It is so hurtful to hear you talk this way. Yes, things have been stressful, but the children have been chipping in and the neighbors have been assisting on a regular basis. We *can* manage all of this without you right now, but what I can't handle is your mood swings. One minute you are your usual self and the next you are in your own world and won't talk to anyone. I know that you are going through a difficult time, but so am I and when you withdraw from me I feel so angry at you. I know

that I shouldn't react this way, but we've always supported each other through difficult times and now you are making yourself unavailable. That's not fair. I've talked to you about this in the past and you just seem to ignore me. I don't want to feel like an outsider looking in!

Amy: Steve, before you respond to Annie, I want you both to know that these issues are very common among couples. Annie, it must have been hard to say all of that and you expressed yourself very well. What I hear you saying is that Steve is not a burden and your wish is for him to get better. In the meantime, you are acknowledging that life has been stressful and that you can continue to handle the demands placed upon the entire family, but you are struggling with how Steve is coping with his present circumstances. Further, if I am hearing you right, you miss his support and ability to comfort you when things upset you.

Annie: (*tearful*) Yes, that is how I am feeling. I just want my husband back. I miss talking to him, snuggling with him, even having sex with him. He doesn't want to be intimate with me at all and even just holding my hand seems too much for him right now. I am trying to be understanding but I am instead growing more resentful by the day. What is wrong with me? I must sound like a complete bitch!

Amy: You do not sound at all like a bitch and before I respond to your comments, I would like to hear what Steve is thinking.

Steve: Annie, I miss you too and I had no idea that you have been feeling all of this. I suppose you're right. I *have* been retreating emotionally, because I

feel so lost and depressed. I lie there on the couch
watching my family proceed with everyday life and
it's as if I am already dead and gone, because I am not
able to participate. I don't know how to be "happy"
knowing that my days are most likely numbered and
I don't want to leave you and the children. I don't
want to leave you! All the nausea, pain and lethargy
have robbed me of the need to have sex or to be close
in general. I'm sorry.

Annie: Now I feel awful saying all of that to you. I
know that you are not capable of doing regular things
right now, but if your days *are* numbered I want to
have quality time with you and the family versus no
time at all.

Amy: You are both making valid points and it is often
difficult to understand a loved one's viewpoint when
both parties are struggling. I am so glad that we met
today, because sharing these feelings is vital to being
able to support each other while going forward. All of
this is very hard and I admire the love that you have
for each other. I again want to reassure you both that
these issues are experienced by so many others in
similar situations.

Annie: I agree that this has been helpful and I feel
much better, but I don't want Steve to give up or feel
like we would be better off without him. That is the
furthest thing from the truth and we all want him to
continue to fight for his life. (*looking at her husband*)
I love you, Steve. What can I be doing differently to
support you better?

Steve: Thank you; I love you too. I just need you to
understand how hard all of this is for me and that
there's nothing more that I'd rather be doing than

helping you with everything. I miss you too and will
be more mindful of my moods and how I handle my
feelings.

Steve and Annie's struggles are very normal and typical. Sometimes
the missing link to making sense out of all of it is to communicate with
one another. It sounds easy, but it is one of the hardest things to accomplish sometimes. A third party (e.g., a therapist) may be very helpful
when emotions run high. Steve and Annie revealed things to each other
of which both were not aware. Sharing this information made room for
more sensitivity and compassion for each other and eliminated the possibility of regrets.

Additional Changes

Role reversals are not the only changes that can occur when there is a
terminally ill spouse. Here are further relationship areas where partners
dealing with a life-threatening illness may experience change:

- **Intimacy:** Stress changes the level of closeness in a relationship. Add to that a spouse who is not well (both physically and emotionally), changes in roles, unpredictable schedules and your own emotions. Understandably, physical and emotional closeness are pushed aside. It can be a subtle or abrupt change.

  Previously, your relationship may have relied on your ability to comfort and "hold" each other during good and bad times, but suddenly you feel alone and isolated. This is a completely normal and common reaction.

- **Adapting:** Change takes time for patients and caregivers to adjust to. People usually feel a sense of loss of control, anxiety, insecurity and fear when faced with change. Your daily routine will be different now and it will become more settled through trial and error. Continue to take deep breaths and remember it's okay to cry. You have been taken out of your comfort zone and it is normal to feel upset and discomfort when adapting to the changes a life-threatening illness brings.

During times of uncertainty and change, things quickly get disorganized and can feel scattered. The world around you feels uncomfortable and as though it is "closing in," because time and emotions do not allow space for de-cluttering. Refer to chapter eight on self-care, because it reinforces the need to accept help from others and to delegate. Remember, with the different treatments, the care of your spouse and the many challenges you must meet, you will need help from others. It is important that you accept gestures of kindness.

- **Communication**: People are not always predictable when they are facing life-threatening circumstances. Both you and your spouse may find yourselves acting out of character. Getting familiar with more and/or less communication will be an adjustment. Remember, you cannot control how your spouse handles this crisis. You can only control yourself and your feelings.

Many caregivers tell me that they feel like they "walk on eggshells" around their terminally ill spouses, because they don't want to say anything that may upset their loved ones. Both of you need to be more sensitive to each other's needs and wishes during this time, but withholding due to fear is not healthy. If you, the caregiver, are struggling with the unfortunate diagnosis, it has been my experience that your spouse probably is as well. He or she may have a desire to talk about the illness but may be hesitating in order to protect you. To remain strong, relationships cannot get through difficult times without open communication. You may be the *only* person with whom your spouse will share his or her feelings, so whatever conversations you can generate may be very therapeutic. Both of you will be trying to learn new ways to communicate, so be gentle with yourself, take deep breaths and keep trying.

Effective Communication

The art of having successful communication is to use "I" statements versus "you" statements. Own your feelings rather than displacing them onto your spouse. Miscommunication often occurs when the other person feels accused or blamed. Here are some "you" statements with corresponding "I" statements for comparison:

A. "You never talk to me about how you are feeling and I know that you are scared. You used to tell me when things bothered you. I guess that you don't need me anymore."

B. "I am feeling overwhelmed and scared right now. I don't know if you can relate, but I'd really like to share with you."

In example A, the statements may make the receiver feel defensive, because the messenger is suggesting that the spouse is not attending to the speaker's needs and the speaker is forced to take care of the spouse.

Example B is a more appropriate way to have effective communication between two people under difficult circumstances, because the messenger is talking about his or her feelings only. The messenger is not casting blame or requesting anything back other than the spouse's attention.

Here are two other examples of a couple communicating their emotions; in the first, the emotions simmer under the surface of the words:

C. "I am going to the store to get food for *your* parents and then to the pharmacy to get *your* medicine. Dinner will not be on time, because I also need to pick up the kids from their after-school activities. Your parents had better not complain! Everyone is going to have to deal."

D. "I am feeling stretched too thin right now and something has to give. My priority is to be available to help you and I know how important it is for your parents to come visit as well. I'm going to make things easy and order pizza tonight and take the neighbors up on their offer to pick the kids up from their after-school activities."

In example C, the caregiver feels resentful that everything is falling on him or her to take care of. Further, the caregiver resorts to displacing his or her feelings onto the spouse by emphasizing that the caregiver is doing everything for the spouse. If the spouse wasn't feeling like a burden before, he or she probably is now!

Example D has the caregiver owning his or her feelings, expressing them in a non-threatening manner and exhibiting self-care by making adjustments to the schedule and accepting help from others.

Remember, you can only control your end of the communication process. I often witness terminally ill spouses who displace their feelings on their partners. While your role should not consist of being a target for the angry, agonized feelings of a loved one who has a life-limiting illness, try not to personalize negative comments directed at you. Your spouse is most likely very frightened and is probably having a hard time handling not only the physical but also the emotional aspects of his or her life-threatening illness.

I encourage one or both of you to seek help if the communication gap becomes destructive to your relationship. A therapist or support group can be very helpful as you redefine roles and can improve the manner in which feelings are communicated and information is given and received between the two of you.

He Needs Help—Or Does He?

Many caregivers ask to speak to me without their spouses present, because they are worried about their spouses' inability to cope with being terminally ill. "Can you give me some examples of what you mean?" I ask them. The most common reply that I hear is, "He doesn't want to talk about his illness at all."

Just because some individuals prefer not to talk about their feelings doesn't mean that they aren't coping with their circumstances. Often, if the person was introverted and reserved prior to becoming ill, he or she will still have these traits after being diagnosed with a life-threatening illness.

Caregivers, families and physicians have often asked me to provide counseling to patients who have life-limiting illnesses out of concern that they are in denial. "What is making you think that she isn't dealing with or accepting her illness?" I ask. The reply that I commonly receive is, "She acts like nothing is wrong, doesn't talk about her feelings and never asks any questions."

The majority of the time I conclude that the ill person is not in denial and is fully aware of his or her current medical issues but has chosen to handle things in a way that meets his or her needs. People inherently "know" that they are sick and they also know when things aren't going well within their own bodies.

Retirement Years

Many older couples I have met have worked hard and raised families only to have the words, "You have a life-threatening illness" put a halt to the planned retirement they have been waiting so long to enjoy. Having been given a diagnosis that one of them is seriously and perhaps fatally ill, they must readjust their hopes and future plans and accept the reality that faces them.

Changes in roles can be particularly challenging at this stage of life. There is a natural depletion of stamina and energy as we progress into our older years and now one partner must care for the ill one. You may be physically fit and quite capable or perhaps you too have health issues that need attention. Do not put your needs on hold right now even though your partner's needs must also be attended to.

Jane and Bill's Story

Jane and Bill, married for forty-five years, had recently purchased a home in Florida where they were planning to move in six months. They had both worked full-time jobs until recently, had four grown children and seven wonderful grandchildren.

Jane was a diabetic and had a long history of depression. Both health concerns were managed well over the years, because she had always taken her medications carefully and gone to her doctors' appointments. That all changed, though, once Jane learned that Bill had suffered a massive heart attack. Despite her adult children expressing concerns about her health, Jane insisted on remaining at her husband's side in his hospital room day after day. She dismissed their concerns and explained that "she was fine" and did not have the time to attend her own doctors' appointments and needs.

Unfortunately, Bill's health declined quickly and what was to be a brief hospital stay extended to several weeks due to his increasing shortness of breath and pain. As a result, Jane's bedside vigil and worry grew more intense until one day she collapsed and was rushed to the hospital's emergency room. Her condition could not be stabilized and she had to be admitted to one of the hospital's medical units. Jane's anxiety rose, because she knew that she was missing out on quality time that she wanted to have with her husband. Sadly, Jane passed away unexpectedly from complications related to her diabetes (which could have been prevented had she attended to her health needs when her family expressed concern). Bill passed away a week later.

Many caregivers express that they only feel a sense of control if they can keep their eyes on their seriously ill loved ones and remain "present." I understand this need and I am the first person to advocate to the medical team that people should not be forced to leave a loved one's hospital room. But there are exceptions to this. When it comes to a caregiver's mental and physical well-being, attention must be paid to his or her own needs. Jane's health issues were exacerbated due to prolonged stress, poor nutrition and lost rest. If the medical team had met with her and ensured, to the best of their ability, that Bill's condition at that time was stable, they could have provided her with the emotional support to empower her to leave her husband's side, if only for a few hours or even a few days, so she could have attended to her own health issues. As a caregiver, you do not want your own health issues to become dire and life-threatening. Please take care of your own body and health issues so that they will not become major problems.

Grieving in the Present

As described earlier, many couples discover that their golden years are about to go off course from what they had originally mapped out. When this happens, anger is one of the most common reactions that I witness from patients and their spouses. The feeling of anger, in my experience, is more prevalent than shock, denial or sadness when learning of a life-threatening diagnosis in the later years of life. Other emotions emerge as time goes on, but initially there is a sense of "being robbed." For example, a typical reaction to learning a spouse has a life-limiting illness in the retirement years may be similar to Steve's:

> I have worked hard my entire life and just when we
> were ready to move to Florida, Carol, my wife, tells
> me she has cancer. I'm so furious! I have been waiting
> many years for us both to enjoy our golden years,
> the fruit of all our labor, and for what? Nothing! The
> person I love will not be here to share this time with
> me. The hell with it all.

Steve's right. Life can be unfair! He has a right to be angry. What a misfortune for him and his wife to have worked and saved for a future that is not to be. However, he and other caregivers must experience and convey the anger from within in constructive ways, because it *must* be worked through. This, too, will be a process which will take time.

You and your seriously ill spouse are both grieving over lost dreams and expectations for what was supposed to be. Everyone grieves differently and it is necessary to grieve so that you can move forward with the next chapter in your lives.

You may be completely focused on what is being medically advised right now, but your spouse may be "stuck" in the anger from life and plans being interrupted. This can leave you in two different stages, so try to be patient. Emotionally it may be easier for your spouse to focus on the anger than it is to accept his or her life-limiting illness right now. This is what he or she has control over for the time being and it is okay.

Providing emotional support to you and your family during such a difficult time is addressed in other chapters, so I encourage you to review them, because you need to know that you are not alone during this time.

Telling Your Life Story

Many patients and caregivers begin to question the meaning of their lives when faced with a life-limiting illness. Retirement years are a time when people begin to look back at what they've accomplished, review the good times and what they've overcome and perhaps how their children have progressed through time.

You and your spouse may be grieving missed opportunities for "what was to be," but the road leading up to this point has been paved with many wonderful events and memories that need to be remembered. Talk to each other about those moments.

When I meet with patients and their caregivers, I ask many questions pertaining to their past and present personal lives. The questions and the answers are for everyone's benefit, not just mine. You and your spouse have a unique history and hearing it spoken out loud validates its importance. In the next case study I asked Mary and Tom, the couple with whom I met, questions which were designed to give me a better understanding of what the couple's sudden "thud" (new cancer diagnosis) was interrupting in their lives and allowed me to see a "snapshot" of their story. There were several purposes for this meeting:

- Did they understand the diagnosis and what the plan was to be going forward?
- How have they coped with difficult situations in the past, both as individuals and as a couple?
- What has or has not been helpful in the past in coping with difficult events?
- Do they have "unfinished business" (i.e., regrets from the past) and how will that influence their current circumstances?
- What was the story of their life together?

Mary and Tom's Story

Mary, a sixty-two-year-old, was diagnosed with congestive heart failure. She and her husband, Tom, were referred to me for supportive counseling. During our first meeting I asked them a series of questions to gain a better understanding of what was presently being interrupted in their lives, to determine what supports might be helpful going forward and to help them value the past and present.

Mary told of their life together:

> My husband and I have been married for thirty-seven years. We have three grown children and six beautiful grandchildren. We actually had seven children, but one died at birth. That was a difficult time in our lives, but we got through it.
>
> How we met is a funny story. Tom's sister was one of my friends when I was a teenager and she took it upon herself to secretly "set us up." She and I decided to see a movie and went to the theater. She failed to mention that her older brother, Tom, would be joining us. I was *not* amused by her little trick, but after spending an evening with him, I knew that she had made the right choice. Tom and I kept seeing each other and we married and have been a close couple through our years together.

Early in their married life one of their children died. The death of their infant was the most difficult thing they had endured together until this point and both became tearful while explaining the details of what had occurred. Mary and Tom spoke about the emotional pain created by this loss and although they will never forget their child, they have moved forward.

Mary and Tom have both been very involved with their children's lives throughout the years and learned early on how to balance family life with work. They described their family as close and always supportive of one another during times of crisis.

Faith has played a strong role in their lives and they remain very spiritual people. Both explained that they would like to make more of an effort to attend services on Sundays and that they remain hopeful that the future will be bright through prayer and good medicine.

The couple also attributed their ability to communicate and support one another as a major contributor to how they have overcome obstacles throughout their marriage and they were quick to point out that they have had their share of low moments. They explained further that commitment and hard work were the two key ingredients that have kept them together.

They have raised three very successful children, all of whom obtained college degrees, have careers and are married with children. Mary and Tom enjoy spending time with their grandchildren and value the quality time that they consistently get with their family.

Both have their share of regrets. Tom wishes he had spent more time with his parents during their final years of life and recognizes now that his priorities were not focused on "quality time" with them. Mary regrets never making amends with one of her sisters whom she became estranged from over what now seems a silly disagreement. Her sister passed away several years ago and Mary never got a chance to say goodbye.

Although Tom and Mary talk openly with each other, each copes differently with major issues. Mary becomes more reserved and seeks personal space whereas Tom prefers to keep his mind active (as a form of distraction from what is bothering him) and spends his leisure time playing golf.

When I asked how they were coping with the recent news of Mary's illness, both became tearful and expressed that they were holding on to hope. They appeared to understand the medical issues, were motivated to pursue treatment and hoped for a bright future while remaining realistic that things might not turn out in their favor.

As we spoke, I was honored that they shared many private and personal details of their lives with me. There were moments of laughter and tears as they spoke about the decades of memories that led to this point in their lives. I now had a sense of who Tom and Mary were and how to help them through this difficult time coping with Mary's life-threatening illness.

We all need to know that our lives make a difference and it can be easy to lose sight of that when faced with a life-threatening illness. Finding purpose gives people a reason to face the serious challenges of a major illness and move forward.

People are appropriately scared when they learn of their loved ones' debilitating illnesses and some express their feelings better than others. Sharing details of their lives is very therapeutic and often allows individuals to release pent-up emotions as they relive the highs and lows of their lives through a life review. I encourage you to do this with your ill loved one. Tears and laughter are welcome! Life still has its lighter moments and it is acceptable to smile and make jokes throughout the journey.

Difficulty Coping

Many caregivers feel at a complete loss and have a sense of helplessness, because their spouses don't appear to be coping well (if at all) with their current illnesses. A person's life story helps clinicians and caregivers understand how the past may be influencing the present and can provide a sense of direction for how to help the patient and caregiver. Fear and anxiety are strong emotions and although you may recognize your spouse physically, he or she may seem a stranger emotionally. This is normal and, for many patients, part of the process toward trying to accept what is happening.

Edward's Story

Edward is a married forty-three-year-old and has a two-year-old son. He suffered a brain aneurism while working out at the local gym. Employed as a computer programmer, Edward was the primary caretaker of his son, because his wife was an airline attendant who was out of town several days a month. It was a routine that had worked well for them until their roles were forced to change.

I received a phone call from Edward's wife, who was having a difficult time coping with her husband's "change in mood" since his diagnosis.

She described her spouse as now being easily agitated, angry and withdrawn from their son. She was tearful and felt completely lost. I arranged to meet with the couple.

One of my priorities in our first meeting was to conduct a life review in order to understand how best to help Edward and his wife. (Please note that steroids are often prescribed to patients with brain trauma in an attempt to reduce swelling and one of the side effects can be severe mood changes. However, I learned prior to meeting with Edward that he was not taking any steroids prior to or during the time surrounding our meeting.)

Edward expressed a clear understanding of what his diagnosis was and showed little emotion while explaining the details. He was brief, very matter-of-fact and logical about what the medical plan was to be going forward. I noticed he did not seem comfortable making eye contact and often looked to the side of the room when speaking.

As a clinician I am trained to follow the lead of a patient. If I "push" a patient such as Edward to discuss things that make him uncomfortable, I run the risk of having him shut down conversation. His nonverbal body language suggested to me that he was a private person who didn't easily share his emotions and that obtaining information was going to be like "walking on eggshells." Edward and I first met alone and I spoke quietly of why we were getting together.

> **Amy:** I would like to begin by telling you that I am sorry to be meeting you under these circumstances. I cannot tell you that I understand what you are going through. What I can connect with is the immense loss of control that you must be experiencing.
>
> **Edward:** (*nodding his head in agreement*) Yes, I am certainly feeling very much out of control right now.
>
> **Amy:** I would like to help you regain some control and the best way that I know how to do that is to gain a better understanding of who you are. So, if it's okay with you, I would like to ask you some questions.

Edward: That would be fine.

Amy: Life as you know it has just been stopped abruptly. What is being interrupted in your life?

Edward: Everything! I am not able to be at work and we can't survive without my income. The physician explained that it is not clear when I will be able to return to work. My wife is an airline attendant and is required to fly out of town several days a month and I am the sole care provider for our two-year-old son when she is away. We do not have any family in the area to help with childcare and I don't know how we are going to manage. Basically, we are screwed!

Amy: I certainly appreciate the stress that this is placing on you, so let's discuss possible options to give you a better sense of control. What was your employer's reaction when you told him that you were sick?

Edward: He was very understanding and told me to take as much time as I need. My boss assured me that he will keep my position open, but he can't continue to pay me once my sick time runs out. I do have short- and long-term disability, so I should be okay, but I don't trust them. "Out of sight, out of mind." And someone has to get the job done if I can't.

Amy: Your concerns are valid and I am happy to write a letter of support to your employer if you think that would be helpful. Over the years it has been my experience that many companies do hold positions for their employees if they've stated as such. You must be a dedicated and well-liked individual at your company, Edward.

Edward: I work very hard for my company and my main concern is to make sure that I can continue to provide for my family despite my illness.

Amy: Your job security sounds fairly solid right now. I want to point out that you have now acquired a new full-time position, which is to fight for your life. The goal is to get treatment and to focus on your health so that you can be around to support your family in the future. I am giving you permission to place all of your energy into focusing on the treatment and allow your wife, family and friends to provide some assistance.

Edward: I understand what you are saying and I will do the best that I can. I am so angry that this is happening to me. I constantly feel like punching a wall.

Amy: Feelings related to loss of control can have that effect and anger is an emotion that is common when things around us feel out of sorts. How have you handled difficult situations in the past?

Edward: Not like this, that's for sure. I have always been able to handle adversity. My father was an alcoholic and abused my mother emotionally. I kept to myself. I have never needed anything from anyone before and I do not want to need anything now!

Amy: Are your parents still alive?

Edward: No, and I was an only child.

Amy: I admire your inner strength, given the environment that you grew up in, but I will suggest that it's not that you never needed from anyone before, rather that you learned quickly that your needs were not going to be met and you protected yourself by putting up walls. In my opinion, you are a survivor! Not only did you move forward in your life, but also you achieved success in the workplace and have been able to form healthy relationships within your immediate family. What do you think helped you to cope with the past?

Edward: I am not sure what has helped me cope, to be honest. I put all of my energy into school and sports growing up and I've been fortunate to have had wonderful mentors along the way who paid more attention to me than my own parents.

Amy: Have you ever sought counseling?

Edward: No, I was and I still am fine. My parents taught me what type of spouse and parent I don't want to be and, until this point, I have done well.

Amy: What do you perceive to be different about how you are acting now?

Edward: I feel so angry that I find myself snapping at my wife and son. I try to control it, but it comes from nowhere. It's best that I stay clear of them as much as possible right now.

Amy: I want to share with you that everything that you are saying is completely normal and, as much as you've "protected" yourself from the past, this new event is stirring up your pushed-down emotions from the past. You can't control your anger right now, because you don't understand where it's coming from.

You are welcome to disagree with me, but you have just found out that you have a life-threatening illness that has made you feel a sense of loss of control that you probably haven't felt since you were a boy trying to survive in your difficult home life. The current issues are unraveling the past issues that a helpless boy did not know how to manage other than to work it out through sports and school.

Edward: (*tearful*) I never would have connected the two situations, but you are so on target. I am feeling so much rage!

Amy: Understanding how past events can influence current events is vital to your being able to regain a sense of control right now.

This was a pivotal moment for Edward and, as my meetings with him continued over time, he was able to work through some issues from the past, which allowed him to be "present" and receive support from his family to deal with his life-threatening diagnosis.

As the spouse dealing with a loved one who, like Edward, has been told he has a life-threatening condition, your situation can indeed make you feel like you are "walking on eggshells." You have been thrown into the role of full-time caregiver and although you can perform that role with much love and compassion, nothing could have prepared you for the endless days of pain, discomfort and living with a spouse who is most likely depressed. Through no fault of your own, a host of mixed feelings are present at any given time.

Caregivers often feel like they are treading on fragile terrain when their spouses act very differently under stress. Being afraid to move forward often leaves the caregiver feeling defenseless and vulnerable.

Perhaps your spouse feels frightened of the future and turns that fear toward you by acting anxious and enraged. But know that your spouse is lucky to have you in his or her life, because you are providing invaluable support by being present. If you are experiencing a serious change in your spouse's mood or personality, as demonstrated in Edward's story, seek help from a therapist and/or support group. Be aware that the changes you are witnessing are due to fear and loss of control. If your spouse declines the support, go alone. Let me repeat again perhaps the most important advice for caregivers: You cannot take care of others if you do not take care of yourself! Take a deep breath and be patient, because the partner whom you know and love *will* reappear. This change is part of the process of coming to terms with such a debilitating diagnosis.

Topics for Reflection

1. How have the roles changed between you and your spouse? If these changes are making you feel overwhelmed, resentful, exhausted or sad, know that this is normal. It is okay to ask for help!

2. What has changed for you in reference to physical and/or emotional needs since your loved one has become sick? Do you have any insight into how you may broach these topics with your partner? There may not be a simple solution to your concerns but communicating can be very relieving.

3. Are you grieving the life that you shared with your partner prior to his or her diagnosis? Don't feel guilty if you are, because it is only natural to miss the person you knew before the diagnosis. Seek a safe environment to talk about these feelings.

4. What is the life story that you and your spouse would tell others? Reflect on the years of memories that you've made together. Talk about them with each other and others. It's okay to laugh and cry.

5. What emotions are you feeling today?

6. What have you done for yourself lately?

Chapter 11

Caring for a Parent with a Life-Threatening Illness

Whether your childhood hero was imaginary or real, there have always been those who appear to be larger than life. Those people inspire us, appeal to our aspirations and help us believe that anything is possible if we try. For many of us, our "superheroes" were ordinary people who did extraordinary things. Many would name one or both of their parents as their first "superhuman" heroes. Your parents kept you safe, guided your first steps and softened the falls when you stumbled. Somehow, they anticipated your thoughts and knew when you were happy or sad.

Through the years your needs changed and your parents remained by your side with solutions and many teachable moments which steered you out of harm's way. It may even have appeared at times that there was no issue too great or too small that your parents couldn't handle. They possessed the answers to what seemed like everything. From a child's viewpoint, your parents' flaws were easily disguised by their statures, "grown up" voices and "always in charge" demeanors.

Everyone's story is unique as to how their parents' status evolved from that of superheroes to mere mortals, flaws and all. At some point you began to have more insight into viewing your parents as "regular folks," instead of powerful people who could do no wrong. This shift is normal and necessary in order to achieve individuality and separation.

My most memorable moment occurred one morning while sitting at the breakfast table with my mother. I was looking at her hands, the same hands that comforted, held, scolded and guided me. But on this particular day, everything that I knew about my mother had a different "feel." Her hands looked aged and the firmness that I had recognized to be part of who she was had wrinkles and age spots. Perhaps *she* had gradually been coming to terms with the change in her appearance, but my realization came suddenly and unexpectedly.

I felt incredibly sad at the realization that this strong, outgoing woman was human, as witnessed by the vulnerabilities that had become visible to me on the outside of her body. That breakfast table experience was one of my first reality checks: that neither she nor I could control time moving forward and that one day I would have to come to terms with the ultimate separation. On that day so many years ago, my mother was no longer invincible. She was, instead, a mortal and one day I will have to face the fact that her life, as the rest of ours, will not go on forever.

Parents are not supposed to age or become sick, because they play such a significant role in our lives. We easily assume that they will be suspended in time forever. The reality is that they *do* get sick and often that means that roles change. This can be difficult for everyone.

Changes in Roles

When a parent is diagnosed with a life-threatening illness, it can be particularly difficult to redefine the parent-child roles that have been in place for decades. Imagine showing up to a job that you've had for many years and being told that starting today you are filling a new position without any warning, training, explanation or guidance. I refer to this as "sink or swim" mode. Abrupt changes can create feelings of anxiety, stress and uncertainty.

Your parent experienced similar feelings when told that he or she has a life-threatening illness that will require the help of others to manage all the things that he or she has been doing independently his or her entire adult life.

Understanding Your Parent's Viewpoint

It can be difficult to understand and empathize with a parent's situation facing a life-threatening illness when you feel stressed yourself at learning your mother or father is so very ill. Nevertheless, gaining insight into your parent's viewpoint may help you to assist your parent with a better sense of understanding and compassion during the challenging moments caused by the emotional and physical distress that the parent suffers.

Everyone's situation is unique and many different factors enter into the equation of caregiving. I am going to provide support and guidance related to what I come across often in my clinical practice with patients and caregivers.

Caregivers often experience the same emotions felt by their seriously ill parents but for different reasons:

Caregiver: As a younger or midlife adult whose parent is faced with a life-threatening illness, you most likely have certain demands or obligations placed upon you each day. You may have children with different needs depending on their ages. If employed, you have tasks and deadlines, household chores must still be done and, with these other added obligations, you can be exhausted many times by the end of the day.

Then you receive a phone call from your parent informing you that he or she has a life-threatening illness and suddenly all the demands in your life multiply. Your heart is probably pounding, palms sweating and thoughts scattered, jumping between gearing up for crisis mode and trying to figure out who is going to take care of the many things that you do each day. You might be thinking, *How am I going to meet my parent's needs with my already demanding schedule?* You have now entered the "sandwich generation," meaning you are caught between the needs of your immediate family as well as the needs of a parent.

Parent: At the onset of many life-threatening illnesses, your parent is most likely in late adulthood and the pace of his or her life is much slower than yours. Many senior adults' lives deal with doctors' appointments, errands, socializing with friends, midday naps and longer periods of time spent at home. Whether or not your parent exhibits these traits or is still working, he or she is in a different phase of life from you. Perhaps he or she is downsizing while you are expanding. Your parent is probably "set in his or her ways" and prefers that things remain simple and uncomplicated.

Caregiver's Fear and Anxiety: Ask yourself how you felt after hearing that your parent had a life-threatening illness? Perhaps you felt fearful of what this new diagnosis would mean in reference to his or her well-being and quality of life. Anxiety and fear usually go hand in hand, as most caregivers feel overwhelmed and anxious about what their new roles will entail and how to manage the needs of two households versus one. Many feel like they can't catch their breaths or find a calm moment.

Parent's Fear and Anxiety: When first diagnosed, your parent most likely interpreted the physician's words to mean impending death. Our society is trained to think this way despite many advances in modern medicine. Feelings of sheer panic and fear are often experienced. After overcoming the initial shock, your parent's concerns may have shifted focus to how to maneuver through insurance issues, confusing medical terminology and the complex healthcare system. He or she has reason to be overwhelmed and scared. The complexity of dealing with doctors, medical treatments, surgical needs, multiple tests and procedures, as well as the effect of heavy medication, all suddenly thrust upon your parent can be overwhelming for him or her. He or she is going to need your help.

Caregiver's History of Achieving Independence: Most adults have day-to-day routines which are probably planned out, except for those rare unplanned moments, until they finally get to bed at night. You and your family have set rules of the house and have duties, social and children's activities as well as work and the other obligations which most adults have. This is right where you are supposed to be in this phase of your life. And while you have been independently moving along the life cycle of the period of adulthood you are now in, your parent's illness will require the family dynamics to change. This can be a very difficult time for everyone.

Parent's Need to Maintain Independence: Your parent may be extremely resistant to accepting help from you or other family members. He or she has played the leading role within his or her own life for many years and agreeing to help from others may be a very difficult adjustment. Furthermore, many senior adults still view themselves as their child's caregiver, whatever stage the adult child is in. Any reversal of roles for parents can be hard to acknowledge.

Common Issues

Your parent facing a life-threatening disease may be struggling with many aspects of adjusting to his or her unfortunate situation. Here are some common issues with which your parent may need assistance:

- Understanding the diagnosis and possible treatment plan
- Keeping track of dates and appointments
- Managing medications
- Physical mobility
- Daily living skills (e.g., dressing, bathing, household chores)
- Understanding insurance policies or dealing with a lack of insurance
- Mental health issues (e.g., depression, anxiety, fear, anger, denial)
- Feelings of immense loss of control

Many caregivers struggle with how to provide assistance to their parents who are resistant to their help. Here are some themes and feelings I have witnessed in parents I have assisted who are patients facing life-threatening illness. These suggested responses to parents may help you to cope with your parent's needs, feelings and mindset.

Feeling Like a Burden

Parent: "I do not want to burden my children with my needs."
Caregiver: A helpful way to respond is, "Dad, you are not a burden at all. You have done so much for me over the years and now I want to give some of that back. I want to help, because I love you, not because I feel obligated. You are providing a gift to me by letting me help you right now."

Changing Routines

Parent: "I feel safe maintaining my set routines and environments."
A sudden change may create anxiety which in turn may create a resistance to pursuing medical attention. In your parent's viewpoint, if he or she doesn't acknowledge that something is wrong then he or she will not have to deal with it.
Caregiver: Acknowledge that these feelings may be present and provide reassurance that your parent will not have to walk the journey alone by saying, "Mom, I know that all of a sudden everything is changing and I can only imagine how much loss of control you must be feeling. I am happy to do whatever I can to make things feel more manageable. I don't want you to feel alone during this difficult time."

Employing Outside Help

Parent: Many seriously ill parents do not want strangers in their homes (e.g., home health aides, cleaning crews, neighbors) for several reasons:

- It forces those with life-threatening illnesses to acknowledge their loss of independence and that they can't do certain things for themselves.
- They don't trust others.
- They are not socially comfortable.
- They have always been very private people.
- They are concerned about spending their money for outside services.

Caregiver: Unless you have decided to or already live with your parent, spending all your time at your parent's home is *not* the solution to this situation. Remember, you need to take care of yourself as well as your parent. Here are some important points to discuss in order to come to an alternate resolution:

- Present your parent with options such as rotating family members, friends, church members, volunteers, hiring an aide or asking your parent if he or she is willing to stay with you and other family members on a short-term basis.
- Discuss your concerns related to safety issues.
- Review finances with your parent.
- Contact your State's Department of Aging to inquire about community outreach programs.

Here are some examples of how to convey to your parent your concern regarding your parent's safety and comfort:

- "Mom, I know that you are opposed to having an aide come help you, but I am worried about your safety. You have been mixing up the medications and are a bit unsteady on your feet. I am not here to tell you what to do, but I am concerned that without some extra support you might have an accident or need to be hospitalized for something serious that could have been prevented."
- "Dad, are you open to giving a home aide a try? If you are dissatisfied and want to discuss changing the plan at any point, we can explore other options."
- "Would you be more comfortable in assisted living? There are many nice facilities, apartments and studios available that we can discuss."

These statements are sensitive to the parent's needs, but they convey honest and sincere concern about his or her well-being. The caregiver does not mandate a solution, but rather allows the parent to feel a sense of involvement and control of the situation by asking his or her opinion on different options.

Resisting Help

Parent: "I don't want any form of help from you or a professional. I can take care of myself."

Caregiver: If your parent fits this scenario it is vital that you attempt to assess his or her mental capacity. Does he or she appear to be thinking clearly? If he or she appears to be confused or disoriented, get him or her to the nearest emergency room or contact his or her physician. In this altered state, your parent will not be capable of making rational decisions pertaining to his or her safety and needs during this critical time.

If your parent is competent and thinking clearly, remember that you cannot control others' actions and behaviors. You can only be in control of yourself! Despite your concern and good intentions to offer support, the reality is that your parent has the right to turn down your help.

Many patients push away those who want to help, because it is a form of maintaining a sense of control. If the parent is of sound mind then you must accept what you feel is a bad decision on his or her part. Watching someone whom you love struggle can be incredibly painful. In my years of experience with patients enduring life-threatening illnesses, I have found that through further physical decline, many patients end up accepting help. Do not feel a sense of regret or responsibility should something happen; you attempted to intervene and your competent parent made his or her own choices.

Feeling like a Child

Parent: "I am not a child to be taken care of by my grown children."
Parents who have life-threatening illnesses often feel humiliated about needing assistance for bathing, dressing and going to the bathroom.

Caregiver: Acknowledge these issues with your parent. For example, say, "Mom, it must be hard for you to require help from me, knowing what an independent person you've always been." Getting issues "out in the open" allows your parent to verbalize his or her feelings and will also provide you with opportunities to give additional emotional support. Here are some more suggestions for handling this problem:

- If possible, have a person of the same sex help your parent with intimate issues such as bathing.
- Some people would rather have an aide than accept their grown children's help with these matters.
- Continue to think about different ways that you can consistently give control back to your parent.

Caregiver Resentment and Anger

There aren't always solutions or quick fixes to obtaining the proper care that your parent may need. Perhaps everything has become your responsibility. There are very real limitations that can prevent your parent from getting the support that he or she needs in the home:

- Caregiver resides in another state
- Caregiver must maintain his or her job and can't afford to take time off
- Caregiver has young children whom he or she needs to be home to take care of
- Lack of insurance or a plan that provides minimal coverage
- Financial issues
- Stressful or poor family dynamics
- Lack of community supports
- Resistance from parent

Providing care to your parent can be very challenging for a host of reasons and many caregivers experience feelings of anger and resentment because of the issues they face:

- Lack of help from other family members
- A strained parent-child relationship prior to onset of illness
- Limited support within the healthcare system
- Financial strain
- Lack of support from caregiver's spouse
- History of abuse (substance abuse or otherwise)

Until our healthcare system changes in order to provide the appropriate support needed to maintain people in their homes, caregiving will remain a strain on the family unit.

If other family members aren't stepping up and offering help, I encourage you to hold a family meeting to discuss distribution of needs. Many families are able to come together during difficult times while others are not. Some family members will be content to allow you to be the one and only caregiver.

I recommend asking for help from other family members if you have not yet done so. Involving other siblings and relatives will bolster your own strength in handling the many needs of a very sick parent, instead of shouldering the burden alone and exhausting yourself so that you cannot meet your own needs and obligations.

If you are unable to acquire assistance from other family members despite reaching out for help, then know that your parent is very lucky, because you are making sure that he or she is not alone during what is a very difficult time. You are most likely enhancing your parent's quality of life and you may be preventing him or her from having to be placed in a nursing home.

Caregiver's Guilt

No one can say how long this journey will last. Often, the most difficult part of the process is not knowing when the journey will end. The role of being a caregiver to your parent who has a life-threatening illness could last for months or years.

If you are secretly wishing that the journey would end sooner than later, know that you are not alone with these thoughts. The majority of caregivers with whom I work are not able to afford additional help for their parents, are living paycheck to paycheck and are figuring out new ways to get what they need from a broken healthcare system. I talk to *many* caregivers who struggle with guilt over having such feelings. Caregiving is hard work and you are most likely feeling exhausted and drained. That doesn't take away from the love that you have for your parent; it merely reinforces that you are human and have physical and emotional limitations.

It is most important that you find an environment to express your feelings and to get support. Here are some suggestions which you could explore:

- **Individual Therapy:** Being a caregiver can be a full time job, but try to find an hour a week to meet with a therapist or other support person to vent your feelings to someone outside of your family. I have learned from my work with caregivers that the relief you will experience will be worth your time. It will also recharge some of your depleted energy.

  If you are struggling with internal anger, resentment or unresolved issues with your parent, therapy is the place to work through these feelings. Taking care of a seriously ill parent can often stir up emotions that have existed within the relationship. There may be issues from the past or guilt over missed opportunities. Individual therapy is most helpful if you are struggling with unresolved issues from the past that are affecting you in the present. Working through some of these issues may help you become more emotionally present with your parent. Obtaining support through therapy may also enable you and your parent to say things that wouldn't have been said otherwise.

- **Support Groups:** Another avenue to receiving help is through support groups. You will be surrounded by others who truly understand what you are going through and it will help reinforce that you are not alone in your struggles.

Katherine and Joan's Story

Joan, a seventy-year-old woman, was newly diagnosed with leukemia when I met with her and her daughter Katherine. Both had many questions about what their needs would be going forward and they appeared to be anxious about financial and logistical issues.

Joan lived four hours away from the hospital where she was to have treatments. She would need to stay locally for approximately twelve months and would also need to have a twenty-four-hour-a-day caregiver due to possible side effects that could occur from the treatment that she would be receiving. Furthermore, Joan would need transportation back and forth to the hospital three to four times a week for blood work and monitoring.

Social Supports

Joan, a retired seamstress, had been a widow for ten years, lived by herself and had two grown children. Her daughter, Katherine, lived near the hospital at which she was to be treated and her son, Andy, resided out of state.

Past Personal History

Joan was a Holocaust survivor. Her aunt and uncle were able to get her and her brother safely out of Germany, but sadly, her parents and extended family remained there and did not survive. Joan reported that she and her brother had to learn survival skills early in their lives and that she had endured a significant amount of emotional pain. She further stated that she had to work very hard for everything that she had achieved in her life.

Counseling

I met with Joan and her daughter Katherine many times over the course of a year, both together and separately. There were several recurring themes that came up during our time together:

Katherine consistently struggled with feelings of resentment and anger. She explained that she and her brother had a good upbringing and that her parents appeared to be happily married. They weren't a family that had a lot of money, but their needs were always met. However, Katherine described her mother as being the authoritative figure and that she could be very strict at times. Her mother did not show much emotion and rarely talked about her traumatic childhood.

Katherine said that she had always known that her mother loved her, but Katherine was often a victim of her mother's criticism and comments of disapproval, which she learned to ignore. Over the years, unspoken tension built between mother and daughter and created emotional distance within the relationship.

Joan's medical team stressed the importance of remaining close to the hospital in order to start treatment. Without hesitation, Katherine, her husband and her children encouraged Joan to stay with them. Joan, feeling as if she had no other choice, accepted.

The journey was complicated both medically and emotionally. Katherine arrived at the hospital each morning at 8:30 A.M. to be with her mother. Day after day, week after week, she attended to her mother's needs. The complex dynamics between mother and daughter became clearer as the emotional and physical toll began to show on Katherine's body and face.

Joan was scared and didn't want her daughter to miss a visitation day at the hospital. Whenever I met with Joan and Katherine they appeared to be comfortable with each other's company. However, over time I began to notice interactions that perhaps represented a more realistic picture of their relationship: Joan often disagreed with her daughter's words, made critical comments about Katherine's appearance and did not acknowledge Katherine's family and obligations that were being interrupted each day.

Katherine was torn between caring for her mother and attending to her husband and children. Despite my many suggestions for her to take off a few days from the hospital visits in order to rest, she would not. I met with Joan and Katherine on several occasions to help them both recognize this need and despite obtaining agreement from her mother to forgo visiting once in a while, Katherine felt guilt-ridden after skipping just one visit.

Often Katherine spoke of her anger and resentment about having to be a full-time caregiver to her mother, whom Katherine felt was ungrateful and had unrealistic expectations of her.

I provided Katherine with support and encouragement to work toward achieving self-care and also provided her with resources to gain additional support. Despite her intentions to follow through, she never did, and her anger continued to grow. As a therapist, I can attempt to provide support to the best of my ability in the present, but I cannot make people do things. Katherine was able to find emotional relief through venting, was often tearful and struggled with the reality that her mother's status was terminal.

Joan was discharged and readmitted to the hospital numerous times during the course of eight months. Meanwhile, Katherine's home life was falling apart and her brother was not willing or capable of providing any support to their mother. Additionally, finances were tight for Katherine and her husband, which made it impossible to hire a home health aide.

Throughout the months, Katherine continued to vent and cry to me while remaining as committed to her mother as she had been when we first met. I often gave Katherine the recognition and praise that she so desperately needed from her mother, which helped to propel her forward. I became the person who provided refueling and served as her crisis management coach. It wasn't an ideal way to achieve support, but it was better than nothing.

The medical team gave Joan the choice on several occasions to stop treatment, enter hospice and focus on her quality of life. Each time she refused and expressed that she would never give up her fight for survival.

Joan passed away after nine months of fighting a very hard battle with leukemia. Katherine was by her mother's side when Joan took her last breath. Unfortunately, Katherine and Joan were never able to talk about their unresolved issues, but Katherine achieved a level of peace knowing that she did everything she could to help her mother through the final year of her life. She did not regret caring for her mother during Joan's terminal illness and hopefully Katherine learned more about herself in the process.

It has been my experience in these twenty years of working with terminally ill patients and their families that the issues which were presented in Katherine and Joan's case are very common among the patients and families with whom I work. The foundation of this mother-daughter relationship was built upon Joan's traumatic childhood events, which most likely had never been dealt with.

Joan was not able to acknowledge her fear; instead, she reverted back to her survival skills of putting on a strong face under incredibly difficult circumstances. In reality, she was grasping at her daughter and asking for help through her abusive tendencies. She also knew that her daughter was not taking care of herself and, in response, Joan clenched even tighter.

As a Holocaust survivor, Joan experienced the loss of her parents under horrible circumstances. They saved her life knowing that they would lose theirs. The guilt and sadness that she experienced over the years crippled her ability to have a healthy and meaningful relationship with her daughter.

Understanding a person's past may help to explain current behaviors, especially when the person is in crisis mode. It does not dismiss everything, but it may help you to attach meaning to a person's actions.

Katherine was able to acknowledge that she was struggling both emotionally and physically, but she did not get further support. Her experience could have been more manageable had she followed through on this suggestion. As I've stressed before, you cannot take care of others if you do not take care of yourself!

Katherine and Joan's story demonstrates what happens when caregivers try to do it all. Katherine tried to juggle the roles of wife, parent and caregiver and she was overwhelmed. It is not only acceptable but also healthy to ask for help.

Setting Limits

We often hurt those whom we love the most, because it is "safer" to verbally unload on family versus outsiders. Many caregivers become verbal punching bags for their seriously ill parents and that is *not* okay. Caregivers are human beings with self-worth and dignity. It is a good idea to seek help if you are having trouble setting boundaries and limits.

An important limit to set is how much time you spend at the hospital with your parent who is facing a life-threatening disease. Patients who are in the hospital are receiving supervision and support twenty-four hours a day. If you are like Katherine and are spending twelve- to sixteen-hour or longer shifts in your parent's hospital room, you will exhaust yourself and burn out. I strongly encourage you to limit your visits to every other day or to just a few hours a day. Additionally, your parent will need a break from you as well in order to sleep, have private time and process his or her thoughts. You need to reserve your energy to meet your parent's needs when he or she is released from the hospital, because this will be when you are the primary caregiver for your parent.

Jenny and William's Story

William, a sixty-five-year-old divorced systems analyst, had three adult children in their forties. He was one of four children and described his immediate and extended family as close. Everyone lived in the same town and got together frequently.

William reported that he had always been in good health, was active and watched what he ate. He was surprised when he noticed bruises on his legs and arms which were accompanied by night sweats that left him soaked. He met with his family doctor, waited for the results of the blood tests and was admitted to the hospital in order to begin emergency treatment for lymphoma.

When I meet with patients and their families for the first time I try to assess the relationship that exists between them. Although I am not meeting them during "normal circumstances," I can often gain a better understanding of how they will cope going forward by paying attention to their body language, eye contact (or lack of it), who dominates the conversation and the emotions (or lack of them) that are displayed.

I met with William and his daughter, Jenny, the day William was admitted to the hospital, knowing that they would be in need of some support dealing with William's sudden and serious diagnosis. Jenny was the oldest of four children, single and in between jobs when we met. I introduced myself to both of them, explained my role and expressed how sorry I was to be meeting them under the circumstances. As I do with any new patient, I asked William what his understanding was of his diagnosis and the medical plan going forward.

William never got a chance to respond, because his daughter answered very quickly for him. In fact, every time I attempted to redirect the conversation back to William, Jenny spoke for him. Since this was my first encounter with them I allowed the dynamics of their relationship to play out, instead of providing interventions which would have permitted William to express himself. He did not appear to be frustrated with his daughter's domineering behavior; instead, he sat quietly and at times stared off in the distance as if he wasn't present at all.

Jenny spoke rapidly and often required redirection back to the topic about which I had inquired. I continued to ask questions in order to gain a better understanding of what their lives were like outside of the hospital and each time Jenny answered for both of them. She also answered questions that only applied to her father such as how he was feeling and how he was coping with the news that he had received.

Having met with all kinds of caregivers, I judged that had I cut Jenny off or forcibly redirected the conversation to her father, I would have more than likely lost the ability to align and connect with her, because she would have displaced her anxiety onto me as the "bad guy." William was listening and I felt, by watching him, that he was digesting my words of comfort during what must have been a very frightening time.

The following day Jenny asked to meet with me alone and expressed that she didn't want the medical team to talk to her father about his illness without her present. She stated that she only wanted positive messages, which conveyed a cure as the only outcome, provided to him. If there was any bad news to be given she wanted it told to her, not her father.

Once Jenny finished her long list of requests, I wanted to gain a better understanding of *her* needs. I asked Jenny to describe her father's personality and what his diagnosis was interrupting for him. Most importantly, I told her how lucky her father was to have a daughter who loved him so deeply.

This hit an emotional chord and through tears Jenny explained that her father had always been her "rock" and that she was "Daddy's little girl" while growing up. Her parents divorced when she was ten and she and her siblings lived with him. She described her siblings as also being very caring and supportive of their father, but, as the oldest, she had assumed the role of primary caregiver.

Jenny went on to describe her father as a quiet and reserved man who had a great sense of humor and would do anything for anyone. He took good care of Jenny and her siblings growing up and she further explained that their needs were always his main priority.

I asked Jenny how her father had handled difficult situations in the past and what his coping skills were.

She described her father as being strong and moving forward during and after stressful events or losses. Jenny had never seen her father cry and although he was a physically demonstrative man who gave many hugs and kisses, he wasn't one to talk about his feelings. Additionally, Jenny felt a strong need to protect him from pain and suffering and she acted as the family gatekeeper in order to buffer any "bad" from coming his way.

I asked Jenny what she thought would happen if her father were to receive bad news in reference to his illness and overall prognosis. Without hesitation Jenny stated, "He will give up." She went on to explain that he had to remain strong and fight, because giving up would not be an option.

I attempted to help Jenny gain some perspective on how her father might be feeling by focusing on the theme of loss of control:

> **Amy:** Imagine how difficult this diagnosis must be for your father to one day think that everything is fine and the next day be told he has a life-threatening illness and has to be admitted to the hospital. His life as he knew it has been completely changed. I can't think of a more loss-of-control situation than not to know whether you will survive an illness.

Jenny, as I said earlier, your father is very fortunate to have you as his daughter and advocate. I can't tell you how many patients I meet who don't have someone to hold their hands and comfort them along the way. Your protective attitude allows me to understand what a wonderful parent your father has been, because you are giving back some of what he has provided to you: unconditional love. I can't tell you that I understand what you are going through, but I can relate to the immense loss of control that you must be feeling right now. We all like things to be predictable and your father's diagnosis is most likely thrusting you into the scary land of the unknown.

Jenny: (*tearful*) You're right. I can't imagine losing my father, so we are going to fight this disease with everything we've got.

Amy: I understand that you are scared over the possibility of losing your father and I want to help both of you regain some sense of control while everything is feeling chaotic. The best way I know how to do that is by providing you with facts. Without realistic information, people cannot make the decisions and choices that are important to them.

Jenny, I know that you want to protect your father by only presenting positive medical updates to him, but please understand that by doing so it will have an opposite effect on his well-being. Try to understand that if you are feeling such a strong sense of loss of control, his has got to be worse.

His life has completely changed. His clothes have been replaced with a hospital gown, his comforts of home have been replaced with four sterile walls and his every move and breath are now being monitored.

The greatest gift that you can give to your father is giving him as much control back as possible, because he is an adult and able to make his own choices about important medical issues that will strongly influence his quality of life. We would not be sparing or protecting him by withholding information; rather, he would be cheated out of being a part of the process. This could leave him with an even greater feeling of loss of control.

Your father is about to take a difficult physical and emotional journey that will have many unpredictable turns. It is his right to hear information along the way and your role is to provide love and support. This is a time in his life when he needs his entire family to support his needs and wishes. If you do so, it is my hope that neither he nor you will look back with a sense of regret.

Jenny, you may not always agree with the choices that your father will make throughout this journey and it is okay to share your opinions with him, but try to keep in mind that ultimately he needs to remain in charge of what is to come, because that is all that he has in his control right now.

I want to share again that I am so impressed with your love and dedication to your father. You have been by his side and making sure that he isn't going through this alone, which may not seem like a lot to you, but, believe me, it means the world to him.

Jenny: I never thought about what is happening to my father from that perspective and now I can appreciate his need to remain in control. I was so caught up in wanting to protect him that I lost sight of his needs.

I have found that many parents facing life-limiting diseases tend to "go along with the plan" that their families think is best, because they don't want to let their families down. There are many times when patients understand that they have a life-threatening illness and that their time is limited, but instead of focusing on their priorities and putting their affairs in order, they endure grueling treatment, because their families cannot accept the reality of the situation and are often in denial. This is why the patient must be a part of the medical decision process from the beginning in order for the patient's needs and wishes to be heard and respected. Once a caregiver's "emotional fog" clears there will be a better sense of peace knowing that the patient's needs have prevailed.

Understandably, caregivers become depleted and, for some, tempers and patience run short. Providing support and care to a critically ill parent while trying to maintain some sense of normalcy is very difficult. The drastic changes to routine necessitated by a life-threatening illness are stressful and often take a toll on both the patient and the caregiver. There are circumstances when caregivers have expectations for how their parents facing life-threatening diseases "should" be acting that are not realistic and may create more harm than good. Some caregivers displace onto their parents their own frustrations and inability to cope with the demands their parents' needs place upon them. Unfortunately, this kind of situation can sometimes cause abuse. There are many possible reasons for such behavior from the caregiver:

- Stress
- Lack of rest
- Lack of self-care
- Family dynamics
- Poor coping skills
- Mental health issues
- Dealing with a complex medical system
- Resentment and anger
- Lack of support
- Pressures from family and employer
- Health issues

Patients and their families spend many hours sitting in waiting rooms, standing in long lines and delayed by traffic jams that make their commutes longer than they should have been. Many patients and their caregivers must endure such problems on a regular basis for many months with no end in sight. At some point we are all guilty of speaking unkind words or exhibiting negative gestures, whether it is with our immediate family, a parent or a stranger. Whatever the reasons may be, I have witnessed caregivers treat their loved ones inappropriately. In order to handle your own difficult role as caregiver, it is important that you remain aware of your reactions during the traumatic period of your parent's life-threatening illness so that you can act appropriately and give the support needed.

The next case is an example of how consistent "wear and tear" can take a toll on caregivers and the price that can be paid by the patient whose ongoing medical treatment and needs depend on the availability of his or her family.

Scott and Thomas's Story

Scott, who was fifty-nine years old, lived by himself and was completely independent prior to becoming sick. When he was diagnosed with Parkinson's disease (PD), he and his physician agreed to a six-week magnetic stimulation treatment coupled with several medications.

Unfortunately, the illness left Scott with physical deficits that made it impossible to do many of his daily living activities and he was also no longer capable of driving a car. Luckily, his ability to process information and think clearly was not yet compromised. Scott's short-term prognosis was favorable, but he required outpatient therapy three times per week. It remained unclear how quickly the disease would progress.

Scott's only child, Thomas, was his primary caregiver and assumed the responsibility of providing daily transportation to Scott's treatments and medical appointments and assisting with Scott's needs at home. Volunteers from their local church provided some help with other tasks, but Thomas took care of the bulk of his father's needs.

I became involved when Scott's medical team expressed concern about how Thomas was treating his father. Thomas was described as being impatient with his father and often placed blame on him for the difficult medical needs and emotional upheaval that they were both experiencing. Thomas expressed his own exasperation that his father wasn't trying to do things for himself, had given up his will to live, needed to eat and drink more and should have a better attitude about his situation. Additionally, Thomas's nonverbal gestures conveyed strong messages to both his father and his father's medical team that he was unhappy with his present role of "caregiver."

Meeting with Thomas, I wanted to gain a better understanding of his responses to the pressure of what was going on and to determine how my help could be useful to both him and his father. He spent our first session explaining that he didn't mind helping his father, if only his father would do more for himself such as walking, eating and spending less time sleeping on the couch in the living room.

Many caregivers assume that their loved ones are capable of doing more and instead are choosing not to, because the caregivers are not familiar with the side effects that can occur from intensive medical treatment such as nausea, drowsiness and joint stiffness. Instead, they view their ill loved ones as being stubborn, lazy or giving up. During my twenty years as a counselor, I have yet to meet a patient who exhibits on purpose the behaviors described by Thomas. In fact, many patients are quite depressed and demoralized, because they can't do the things they used to do for themselves.

Thomas assumed that his father could eat more, so he pressured him during every meal and both men were constantly frustrated with one another. I explained to Thomas that his father's current physical issues were directly related to his disease and treatment. I discussed with Thomas what the realistic and unrealistic expectations were going forward. I also gave emotional support, which allowed Thomas to vent his feelings about being an overwhelmed caregiver.

I didn't get the impression that Thomas was abusive or intentionally trying to mistreat his father. Rather, he felt the need to fix the major problems he saw in his father and had no understanding of the medical issues that his father was experiencing. My role was to help Thomas recognize the true limitations that were beyond his father's control and how to manage his own frustrations:

> **Amy:** Thomas, I can appreciate how frustrating it must be when you want to help your father and he isn't capable of completing certain tasks. Most of us are taught from an early age that we must eat and move to keep our energy up, so it is natural that you want to help your father with these tasks. But these aren't normal circumstances right now and what may come easily to you and I may be extremely difficult for him.
>
> **Thomas:** I am very concerned about my father's lack of will to do more. I want to know how I can get him to be more active and to eat more.
>
> **Amy:** Your father's nausea and drowsiness is very common among patients who have PD. In time his appetite may improve. I want to stress the importance of keeping your father well hydrated, but please understand that people can survive for quite a while without ingesting a lot of calories. In fact, small meals and snacks can be easier to digest.

Thomas struggled with my feedback and continued to insist that his father *needed* to eat whether he had an appetite or not. Seeing in Thomas the frustration and irritation that others have described to me provided me with an opportunity to address his issues and some of his concerns:

> **Amy:** Thomas, you look frustrated right now. I can only imagine how difficult it must be to want to do

everything possible for your father and yet feel completely helpless when he *can't* participate.

Thomas: It's not that my father *can't*, but rather that he *won't* do the tasks. I'm tired of having to treat my father like a three-year-old.

Amy: Have you ever had the type of flu that made every inch of your body ache? The strand of flu that makes you feel like "death"?

Thomas: I have, but I don't understand what that has to do with my father's condition.

Amy: What would have happened had someone suggested the importance of eating while you were suffering from the flu?

Thomas: Oh, I think I understand what you're saying.

Amy: Thomas, your father was a completely independent man prior to his illness and it is important that you allow him to remain in control of certain things in his life while so many issues are feeling out of his control. His mind is still working well, which should allow him to remain in control of making some choices, but even this has been compromised by your need to make those choices for him. You would help his state of mind and confidence a great deal if you allow him to decide on things such as whether or not he wants to eat. Remember, he is not choosing to abstain out of stubbornness, but rather these are real side effects that are limiting his ability to actually carry through with certain tasks.

Thomas, I know how much work and dedication goes into being a caregiver and I am concerned about your well-being too. Burnout sneaks up on caregivers without warning and it can be difficult to remain

patient and understanding when you are depleted of
energy.

I went on to talk to Thomas about the importance of self-care and he
was able to identify his mood swings and behaviors that were not helpful
to his father's situation. I also provided him with resources such as local
support groups and continued to meet with him on a regular basis to provide ongoing emotional support and counseling, which helped him feel
that he was not alone throughout the difficult journey of his father's life-
threatening illness. As a result, Thomas gained a better understanding of
his father's limitations as part of the disease process. This allowed Thomas
to be a more nurturing caregiver.

It is often difficult to understand the reality of a traumatic situation,
such as a loved one's very serious illness, when immersed in the middle
of it trying to help that loved one. Many caregivers are consumed with
attempting to fix things while in crisis mode, versus understanding and
listening to their parents' needs.

Thomas and Scott's story demonstrates some common issues and
themes that occur between caregivers and their parents who are facing
life-threatening diseases:

- The parent's needs and wishes can unfortunately get pushed to
  the side while the caregiver's often unrealistic expectations take
  front and center. Many patients allow their caregivers to "take
  over," because the patients want to please them or are afraid to
  communicate their needs.
- Remember, the journey that you are on with your parent is a
  marathon, not a sprint. Too many caregivers forsake their own
  physical and mental health needs, leaving them tired, frustrated,
  short-tempered and perhaps with a false sense of reality.
- Caregivers also need to take care of themselves.
- Regret is a powerful and often crippling feeling that can be
  avoided when a patient is allowed to voice his or her thoughts.

Remember, speaking up may be one of the few things that remain within your parent's control.

- Caregivers may not always agree with their parents' choices, but it is vital to listen and respect them.
- There *are* supports available for caregivers and it is vital that you contact and use these in order to recharge your emotional and physical energy.

Being a caregiver during a parent's life-threatening illness is a very difficult time in your life. However, despite the frustrations, exhaustion and emotional pain in this chapter of your life, try to remember that you have been afforded the gift of time with your loved one instead of his or her sudden death. Use the time wisely and most importantly, know that you are not alone!

Topics for Reflection

1. What was your relationship like with your parents growing up and how were issues discussed and/or handled? Were you raised in a family that fostered open communication or not? This chapter discussed how open communication between you and your parent will be an important component for ensuring a good quality of life while your parent is sick. If you were raised in a family that did not discuss difficult topics together, I encourage you to take risks, because it is never too late to work on communication skills with those whom we love.

2. As a caregiver, did you identify with any of the issues and case histories discussed in this chapter? If so, which ones and why? Unfortunately, there are no definitive rules, for each case has different needs and issues. But there are many "teachable moments." Take time to reflect on the role that you play and whether or not you have areas that need improvement.

3. List three things that you have put in place to take care of yourself during this stressful time. If you have none, do not delay including some healthy aids and comforting actions in your daily life. Whether

it is taking thirty minutes a day just for you and meditating, exercising, finding a local support group, accepting help that others have been offering to you or just taking a hot bath, begin now to employ these supportive aids for your own well-being.

4. Complete this sentence: "If my parent were gone tomorrow I wish that I would have…" You have the ability to reduce future feelings of regret by saying words and taking actions while your parent is still here. It may be difficult, but it will be worthwhile.

5. Complete this sentence: "My parent's needs and wishes are…" If you are not able to complete this sentence, make some time to talk with your parent and gain a better understanding of what your parent's needs are.

6. Do you have other family members who can be helping you and your parent in this difficult time but aren't? If so, why not? I encourage you to communicate to them that, if you are the primary caregiver, you need their assistance as well.

7. When was the last time that you had a good cry or release of emotions? Give yourself permission to express how you are feeling to yourself or another, write in a journal or talk to a counselor in order to vent how and what you are feeling.

Chapter 12

Progression of Hope

Hope and perseverance are my two favorite words. A goal that may seem unattainable is usually achievable when the sheer will to persevere is present. I am a firm believer that if we put our hearts into achieving our goals, anything is possible.

Hope has many faces and stages for those who are facing life-threatening illnesses (caregivers as well as patients). Keep in mind that ill loved ones and caregivers may experience these stages at different times. There is no right or wrong way to experience hope.

- **Stage One:** When a person is first diagnosed with life-limiting illness, the hope is to be cured. Expectations are high for a full recovery.

- **Stage Two:** Unfortunately, some patients will be provided with updates that indicate that their diseases are not responding to treatments and that despite their physicians' best efforts, they are not curable. The hope then shifts to living as long and as well as possible. Some people are provided with a timeframe (such as six months, one, five or ten years). Physicians provide these estimates based on their experience and past cases. These are not exact timeframes and I have witnessed people who outlive the odds. Having a "sheer will to live" is powerful and often takes a person who has a life-limiting disease beyond predictions.

- **Stage Three:** When patients and families are told that there are only days or weeks left to live, each individual responds differently to this news. At this point, hope shifts to making sure that whatever time your loved one has left is quality time and to ensuring there is no pain or suffering. This is a difficult time.

Some people will be blessed and never have to shift to different phases of hope. Others will be less fortunate.

Your ill loved one's physician will discuss what the goals of treatment are and whether or not your loved one's disease is responding (i.e., the disease is diminishing or remaining stable).

It is very normal that as information is provided, you and your seriously ill loved one will experience emotional changes. Just as there are different examples of what hope can look like, there are different emotional reactions too. People commonly experience feelings of denial, anger, acceptance and perhaps a sense of peace. There is no exact timeline or rule for how people move through these emotions. In fact, it is normal to go back and forth between them.

It is important that you are aware of these emotions. Your challenge as the caregiver is to know how to remain in your supportive role as your and your ill loved one's emotions shift. This can be a daunting task. If the disease advances, your feelings of helplessness may intensify. It can be awful to watch someone you love struggle and not be able to make things better for him or her. Don't, however, underestimate the power of presence. You are giving your loved one the greatest gift possible by making sure that he or she is "not doing this alone." Imagine how much scarier the situation would be if your ill loved one didn't have you.

Here are several things your role as caregiver encompasses at this point:

- Listen. Provide your loved one the space and time that he or she needs to talk about his or her feelings. Listening can be very challenging. Most of us want to fix another's problems and we forget that there are times when a person only needs us to listen.

- Be honest. The physicians and I make a point to give information directly and honestly. Patients and families cannot make choices unless they have the facts. If you hear some unpleasant medical information, don't withhold it from your loved one. Be honest with him or her and do not pretend that everything is going to be okay.
- Support your loved one's goals. Perhaps he or she wants to take a trip or visit people that lack of time has not permitted prior to now.
- Give lots of hugs.
- Allow your loved one to grieve and cry.
- Accept and support your loved one's wishes. It is common for me to hear a patient express that he or she is tired and ready to stop treatment.

Be careful not to fall into the "providing solutions" mode, because this will either create false hope or provide little relief. Here are some examples of creating false hope and getting off the track of being an effective listener:

- "You just have to work harder to keep your strength up. If you would just eat more and get off that couch then your disease will respond to treatment."
- "You have to remain positive. You are not putting enough positive energy into getting better."
- "Everything is going to be okay. You are going to win this battle. Be strong."

These comments may make the caregiver rather than the ill loved one feel better. I encourage you, to the best of your ability, to get more comfortable with silence. Remember: It is your presence and listening skills that are priceless at this time. If your loved one is sharing his or her overwhelmed and sad emotions, here are some better examples of comforting replies:

- "I am truly sorry. I hurt for you and I wish that I could make it better."
- "I am here for you. Is there anything that I can be doing for you to help you feel better?"
- "I am glad that you are getting your feelings out. I would be concerned if I didn't see your emotions, because nobody can hold them in forever. Please know that I am always available to listen."
- "I know this is scary. I'm scared too. I will support whatever you need. I want you to be confident that you are doing everything right. As far as I can tell, you are. You are doing everything that the doctors have asked of you and if I thought that there was more that you could be doing, I'd tell you."
- "I hear you. I can only imagine how tired and frustrated you must be. When you started this journey it was never clear how life-altering it would be. If I can make things easier, tell me. Please know that we are in this together."

If words fail you and you feel as if you are "walking on eggshells," you can never go wrong with a hug. It is also acceptable for you to cry and show your emotions with your loved one. Showing your feelings in front of him or her doesn't make you a less effective caregiver. It shows you love the ill person and want to comfort and be with him or her in these difficult times.

Topics for Reflection

1. It is normal that as new information about the progress of a life-threatening illness is provided, you and your loved one will experience emotional changes.

2. Hope can still be very much present; it has shifted, but it is present. What are you hoping for? What is your loved one hoping for? If you can't answer the second question, ask him or her.

3. Listen effectively, rather than giving in to the urge to lapse into "providing solutions" mode, which can create false hope.

4. Don't withhold unpleasant medical information from your loved one. Allow him or her to make informed decisions, even if this means that his or her stage of hope may shift.

Chapter 13

Preparing for and Adjusting to Hospitalizations

Complex issues can arise when your loved one facing a life-limiting disease is admitted to the hospital. Let's discuss how you as the caregiver can make the hospital stay a more comfortable and less stressful experience.

Feeling loss of control is common when a person becomes a hospital patient. The patient is confined to a hospital room rather than the comfort of his or her home. Additionally, the hospital staff requires the patient to wear hospital-approved clothing, dictates what food the patient will eat, disturbs the patient's sleep periodically to check vital signs and monitors the patient's bodily functions. Treatments can be difficult and energy depleting. In addition, there may be needed surgeries and coping with aftereffects. The experience of being a hospital patient can be overwhelming. Here are some suggestions you can follow to help your loved one gain back some control and comfort while spending a period of time in the hospital:

Bring Pieces of Home to the Hospital

- Bring pajamas for your loved one to wear in the hospital. Hospital gowns can be uncomfortable and too exposing.
- Decorate the hospital room with photos of family and friends. Have children create pictures, poems and posters to hang up.

- Pack your loved one's favorite pillow, blanket and stuffed animal from home.
- Supply a CD/MP3 player, portable DVD player, books, magazines or laptop to help your loved one pass the time.
- Provide a cell phone *with* the charger.
- If there are no food restrictions, bring some home-cooked meals. (Additionally, I encourage you to bring boxes of chocolates and other goodies for the nursing staff. They will appreciate this gesture.)

A Word of Caution When Preparing for Hospitalizations

- Don't bring valuables.
- Handle eyeglasses, hearing aids and dentures carefully. Keep them in safe places and in their proper containers so they are not accidentally mixed in with laundry or another patient's belongings.
- Personal medications cannot be administered in the hospital. Keep them at home. The medical team will ask questions about what was being taken at home and will write new orders according to your loved one's current treatment plan.

Preparing for Surgery

If your loved one's physician recommends surgery, a patient can begin the pre-surgery process up to two weeks before the scheduled surgery date. You and your loved one will be contacted by a member of the team to review medical information and history and to answer questions.

Important items to bring on the day of surgery:

- Medical insurance card
- Orders and forms from your loved one's physician
- A copy of your loved one's Advance Directive, if your loved one has completed one (Make sure to make a copy beforehand, because the hospital will not return this to you.)
- List of current medications

Medical Social Workers

As a medical social worker, I would like to educate you about what we are able to provide for you and your loved one facing a life-limiting disease. Social workers conduct thorough psychosocial assessments in order to determine the needs of the patient and his or her family prior to, during and following a hospitalization.

Illness and hospitalization are stressful for patients and their loved ones. Medical social workers recognize that the relationship between psychosocial factors and illness can influence recovery. Therefore, they help patients and families cope with the social, emotional and financial problems related to illness.

Social workers specialize in adjustment to illness and grief counseling for the patient and the family unit. Furthermore, they can assist with post-hospitalization needs such as placement into a nursing home or rehabilitation center or arranging for home care and/or hospice services.

Medical social workers are primarily advocates. They argue for patients' needs and rights on a regular basis. I recommend highly that if you need assistance, ask for the social worker. If the social worker cannot answer your questions, he or she will help you find someone who can.

Be a Gatekeeper

Relatives and friends will want to visit, but your ill loved one needs you to be the gatekeeper. Ask your loved one each day what his or her wishes are regarding visitors. It is helpful if you act as the gatekeeper, because patients often feel like they need to stay awake and entertain visitors. If visitors do come, explain to them that short visits are appreciated. Some visitors feel compelled to stay for hours, which can be very stressful for both you and your loved one.

Prepare for Visits

Family members may want to visit after hearing that your loved one has been hospitalized with a life-threatening illness. We have discussed how to be an effective gatekeeper and now I want to review helpful topics that you and your loved one should consider in preparation for these visits:

- Hospital visiting hours typically start by 10:00 A.M. (giving the nursing staff time to administer morning medications and help patients with their hygiene needs) and end at 11:00 P.M. Some hospitals don't have set visiting hours at all. Know what the hospital's visiting hours are and communicate these to your family. If your loved one has a preference for visiting times, make sure to share this with family as well.

- Children under age fourteen will need permission to visit from the nursing staff and must be accompanied by an adult. Children tend to harbor colds and germs that can be very dangerous for certain patients.

- If your loved one is in a critical care unit, visitation is usually limited to immediate family members and significant others. Ask a nurse in the unit for the visiting hours, because they can change according to the needs of the unit.

- The Health Insurance Portability and Accountability Act (HIPAA) is a federal privacy rule that took effect in 2003. It gives patients more control over their health information and protection of their personal medical records. If a member of the medical team enters your loved one's hospital room and it isn't clear who the visitors are, the patient and/or caregiver should grant permission for further conversation to proceed or ask the visitors to leave the room. There could be sensitive information and it is your loved one's right to keep that private, unless he or she states otherwise.

Caregiver Self-Care While a Loved One Is in the Hospital

Any stay in a hospital room longer than forty-eight hours can make the room feel stifling and confining. Minutes can feel like hours and there's only so much television watching or reading that a person can do in one day. Caregivers and patients both have to deal with feelings of boredom and restlessness. On the unit where I work, it is common to have some patients stay for thirty or more days, because many of them are receiving chemotherapies that take their blood cell count down to zero. That means that their immune systems are extremely weak and what others may be easily able to fight off (a common cold or the flu) could be dangerous to their health.

Caregivers often have the need to endure these long days and some caregivers choose to spend each night in the hospital room and never leave to go home. These are *not* good examples of self-care and these behaviors will soon leave caregivers feeling exhausted. I understand why caregivers want to be present and there are times when I recommend it, but those times are usually related to a patient declining medically, not because he or she is lonely or bored.

Caregivers must take "time outs" in order to:

- Get rest—The hospital is not a good place to get sleep.
- Attend to responsibilities in the home—When chores pile up, your stress doubles.
- Go to work—If your loved one is physically stable and will be in the hospital for a long period of time, I encourage you to go to work. The stimulation will be good for you and you will need to take time off from work after he or she comes home.
- Exercise—You *need* physical movement. Sitting and staring at your loved one for long periods of time doesn't accomplish anything. Your loved one could most likely use some alone time.
- Eat well-balanced meals—It's difficult to keep your energy up if you aren't attending to your basic needs and food is one of them. The hospital cafeteria may not be able to provide the food that you need. Get out of the hospital to an area where there aren't other patients and families walking around. Have lunch with a friend or simply find a quiet place that has a more relaxing atmosphere.

I have seen many caregivers burn out and I don't want you to fall into this category. Many caregivers feel guilty if they attend to their own needs. If you are struggling with this, speak to a medical social worker.

Talk about your internal conflicts and, together, you can sort these out and even communicate these feelings with your loved one.

Prepare Children for Hospital Visits

Preparing ahead of time for children to visit the hospital is very important. Their emotional reactions to seeing an ill person in an unfamiliar setting will differ depending on age, but the experience can be scary and overwhelming for any child. Some hospitals will not allow a child under age twelve to visit. There also may be limits to visitations during flu season. Here are some hints to make a child's visit to the hospital a positive experience and help keep the child connected with your ill loved one:

- Explain why the loved one is in the hospital, but make it age-appropriate. For example, you might say, "Daddy is in the hospital because of his cancer and he is not feeling well. The doctors and nurses are trying their best to make him feel better."
- Describe the setting, including what a hospital room looks like, what machines might be in place, who works at a hospital, etc.
- Describe what the loved one will look like (e.g., he may have some special tubes coming out of his body, she may be bald, he may get sick to his stomach, she may be very sleepy, he could have some pain, etc.).
- Explain that the child can still kiss and hug the loved one.
- Have the child bring something to keep him or her busy (e.g., paper, markers, video games, books).
- Let the child know it is okay to keep visits short or to take breaks (e.g., take a walk to the cafeteria), because a child may feel overwhelmed or frightened. He or she will probably not be able to voice his or her anxiety. It is your job to monitor the child's mood and actions. The child needs you to take control of the situation for him or her.
- Have the child bring a gift or special object to the hospital that can be left with the loved one when the visit is over. Children often believe in the concept "out of sight, out of mind" and it

can be disturbing for them not to see a parent or other loved one on a regular basis. Explain to the child that he or she has a very important job to do: He or she needs to pick out one of his or her favorite stuffed animals, toys or blankets to leave with the parent or loved one at the hospital. Explain that a piece of him or her will be with the parent or loved one even when he or she can't be there in person. This allows a child to feel connected to his or her loved one even though they have to be separated. The same goal can be achieved by having the child draw pictures to hang on the wall.

When the hospital visit comes to an end, a child may have a difficult time with the transition of having to leave the parent or loved one behind. Tell the child that it is okay to feel sad and to cry, but be careful not to make false promises. Do not tell the child, "Daddy is going to get all better and he will not be sick when he comes home." Instead, say something based on one of these suggestions:

- "Daddy is going to stay here with the doctors and nurses. They are working hard to help him. We will pray that they can help him."
- "Mommy is working really hard at trying to get better so she can come home. I know it is hard to leave today and we will come back soon. In the meantime, your stuffed animal will be keeping an eye on her for you. Mommy told me that it's okay for you to continue to have fun with your friends and to go to school to get really smart. Mommy also told me that she will be keeping you in her heart and will be thinking about you all of the time. You can come to me for as many hugs as you want."

The key points that you want to stress with your child in this discussion are:

- Acknowledge how hard it is to say goodbye.
- Reassure him or her that there will be future visits, if appropriate.

- Remind him or her that a piece of him or her (such as the stuffed animal) will be with the parent or loved one.
- Assure him or her that it is okay for his or her life to go on.
- Indicate that the child and parent or loved one are together in thought and spirit.
- Reiterate that you are there to provide support and hugs.

Depending on his or her age, your child may not be developmentally mature enough to know how to cope or to express his or her feelings and will be experiencing many different emotions, just as you are. Some children may act out, withdraw, become hyper, have physical reactions, etc.

It is important that you "check in" verbally with your child. Ask if he or she has any questions about your loved one or anything related to the current changes that the family is experiencing. Ask about his or her mood (you can use a chart that displays different faces: happy, sad, angry, frustrated, confused, bored, tired, cranky) and help him or her to identify and acknowledge his or her feelings.

If your child is in school, I think that it is important to make the school counselor, teachers and principal aware of the situation at home. They will be able to help monitor your child's mood and coping skills and they will be a consistent source of support for you and your child.

The caregiver often gets sandwiched between the needs of the patient and the needs of the children. You cannot sustain your caregiving role if you don't take care of yourself. If you need to, go to the sections on self-care for reminders on how to take care of yourself.

Topics for Reflection

1. The number one theme when having to be in the hospital is "loss of control." How can you help your loved one who is hospitalized to regain some control?

2. Bring a bit of home to the hospital room (e.g., pictures, blanket, pillow, etc.).

3. Communicate with your children about what is happening. Allow them to visit their loved one in the hospital and be sure to explain what the scene will look like before they arrive.

4. Have your children bring a piece of themselves to be left at the hospital (e.g., stuffed animal, favorite toy).

5. Remember to take care of yourself while all of this is going on.

6. Take good notes and get contact numbers.

7. Ask as many questions as you need to!

8. Allow others to help and support you.

✑ Chapter 14 ✑

Handling Bad News

I hope that you and your loved one will not have to receive the difficult news that despite all attempts to cure or prolong life, there are no
further treatment options for your loved one with the potential for success. The medical team, of which I am a member, strongly believes that the
patient should be made aware of all medical information throughout the
progress of his or her disease. As the caregiver, your love and comfort will
be especially important when this critical time of the journey's end nears.

The caregiver needs to help the patient be a part of the process of
diagnosis from the beginning and this should remain so throughout the
course of the illness. People cannot prepare or make plans to meet their
quality of life needs unless they have all of the information. Having full
information also allows people to feel more in control, even when they
reach the terminal point.

Breaking the ultimate bad news is difficult and painful and, like
much of the journey you've trod, can feel once again like "walking on eggshells." Through the years I have come to believe that a determining factor
as to how someone may respond is the manner in which the information
is presented.

Here are some common reasons why caregivers are reluctant to share
this sad news that death is imminent with their loved ones who have been
facing life-threatening diseases:

- If he knows how sick he is, he will stop fighting and give up.
- She will feel like she has failed us.
- He will feel like his physician has given up on him.
- She will feel like she's being punished.
- He will be upset.
- Her fate is in God's hands. God will take care of her.

These examples demonstrate our innate need to protect those whom we love from emotional pain. I understand that need, but I would like to suggest to you why it is not fair to your loved one when you withhold the critical medical information that treatment is ending:

- It is my belief that a patient already senses that he or she is going to die.
- A patient may have stated his or her wishes in an "advance directive," but these cannot be honored properly if he or she doesn't receive accurate information.
- The patient may decide to stop aggressive treatments that take him or her out of the home, if the patient is informed that the treatments are not improving his or her odds of recovery.
- It may be the patient's wish to spend whatever time he or she has left in the comfort of his or her home surrounded by family.
- The patient may want to put his or her affairs in order.
- The patient may want to say things to people that he or she would not say otherwise, knowing the reality of his or her prognosis.

The most important reason to inform ill loved ones of all medical news, in my opinion, is to prevent a sense of regret. I believe it is important for caregivers to know that they took the time to listen to their loved ones' needs, wants and wishes to the best of their ability. If, in the end, caregivers can look back and believe that there is nothing that they would have done differently based on their loved ones' needs, then it is my hope that the caregivers will have a sense of peace.

Here is an example of a situation that could leave a caregiver with a sense of regret for years:

John's Story

John, in his mid-forties, was diagnosed with an aggressive disease and, despite many months of treatment, was told that it was progressing and not curable. The family encouraged John's primary caregiver, his brother Ted, to ask John's physician, Dr. Morgan, whether or not there were any more medical options left to prolong their loved one's life.

> **Dr. Morgan**: Well, we have an investigational trial that we can try, but this will require frequent trips back and forth to the hospital and the drug may produce side effects that could rob John of good quality time at home. There are no guarantees.
>
> **Ted**: If he tries this drug, how much longer could he have to live?
>
> **Dr. Morgan**: I cannot provide exact numbers, but he could possibly have two to three more months.
>
> **Ted**: John is a fighter. He doesn't give up. Of course he will want to try whatever you have to offer.

Nobody thought at this juncture to ask John what he wanted. Perhaps he was tired of being in and out of the hospital; perhaps he clearly understood the risks versus benefits of stopping treatment. It may have been John's wish to be fully present and available in his home and to spend whatever time he had left with his loved ones.

It is your job as the caregiver to be aware of and support your loved one's needs. Otherwise, the roles can easily become reversed. Your ill loved one may push him or herself to undergo procedures and therapies, because he or she feels an obligation not to "let you down." Your loved one needs your permission to follow his or her instinct and heart. He or she needs to know that you support him or her unconditionally.

It has been my experience that when a patient makes the choice to stop treatments, he or she is coming to terms with his or her own mortality. The patient has usually arrived at a sense of peace that the end of his or her life is approaching.

It is when a patient has obstacles in his or her way (e.g., the family pushes him or her to keep going) that I witness a greater chance that the caregivers are left with regret, because, in hindsight, the patient did not have a peaceful end of life.

Lee and Gloria's Story

Breaking bad news allows for support and removes regret for the caretaker and patient. Lee and Gloria, a married couple, discussed Lee's life-threatening disease with his physician, Dr. Wright, and myself.

> **Dr. Wright**: I wanted to meet with you both today to update you on Lee's medical status and to discuss where we go from here. I would like to ask you, Lee, what is your understanding about your disease and how are you doing emotionally?
>
> **Lee**: I know from our last visit that my disease is advancing and is not curable, but I am hoping that we can discuss whether or not you can offer me an experimental drug that I read about. I have been very tired. I spend most of my day sleeping on the couch and I have experienced a significant amount of pain in my legs recently.
>
> **Dr. Wright**: You are correct about the status of your disease. It is not curable and, in fact, it is progressing at a rapid rate. The current scans reveal that it has spread to your lungs and other organs. There is one experimental drug that I can offer.
>
> **Gloria**: Please tell me what the side effects of this medication will be.
>
> **Dr. Wright**: The possible side effects are increased nausea, weakness and lethargy. He will have to come back and forth to the clinic two to three times per week to have his blood levels checked. It will not

cure him. But it will hopefully give him a few more months to live.

Gloria: (*to Lee*) It sounds like the medication that he is offering may only extend your life a few months and that you will need to spend a significant amount of that time coming back and forth to the clinic. And the side effects may worsen your quality of life. I will support whatever you decide, but I want to make sure that you understand the information that he is presenting. What do you want to do?

Lee: I understand. Given the limited time that I have left, I do not want to go forward with any more forms of treatment. I want to spend time at home with my family, but I don't want to be in pain or suffer.

Dr. Wright: There is no right or wrong way to go forward. I respect your wishes and I will explain to you what supports can be put in place at your home to ensure that you are not experiencing pain and suffering.

Gloria: (*to Lee*) I hear and understand what your wishes are right now. Please know that we will all support the choices that you make.

Lee: (*to Gloria*) I do not want to be a burden to you and the rest of the family. My needs take up so much of your time.

Amy: Lee, your comment is probably one of the most common concerns I hear. Here's what I want to share with you: You married your wife for better or worse. You have been there to support each other throughout this journey and have worked as a team through the highs and lows. What would you say to your wife if she were the one who was sick and expressed concerns about being a burden?

Lee: I would reassure her that she should not feel that way and that I would never feel that she is a burden.

Amy: Lee, the conversations that I have had with you and your wife make it clear that she feels the same way about you. I know that it is difficult to need assistance from your family and I also know that it has been very hard to lose some of your independence. Your family loves you and the reason I know that is because they now want to give back what you have given to them. The greatest gift that you can give to them is to allow them to show their love through actions.

I need to convey to you and your family how sorry that I am that we are talking about this. I wish that I were meeting you when you were well. But since I'm not, I want to make sure that the medical team and your family are doing everything the way you would like it to be done. It remains very important that you are in control of making the decisions and choices that are important to you, with the love and support of your family beside you.

Lee's physician began by asking Lee what his understanding of his disease was. The conversation could have been much more difficult if Lee was under the impression he was responding well to the treatment and had no idea that he was dying. Patients' "will to live" can often obscure their understanding of physicians' updates; when I ask patients to voice what they have heard they often describe completely incorrect interpretations of what physicians have said to them. By having the patient explain his understanding first, the physician or medical team can get a better sense of how to explain further what the patient's options really are. It also allows for the information to be conveyed with more compassion, instead of just blurting out grim news and having the patient experience shock.

Dr. Wright did not hide the reality of the situation. He provided one last treatment option, but he was clear that it would probably only extend Lee's life for a short period of time. Furthermore, the doctor could not guarantee that the benefits would outweigh the risks. Dr. Wright also provided an idea of what the next few weeks or months would be like if Lee wanted to try the new medication. He did not give Lee a sense of false hope.

A crucial thing Dr. Wright provided for the well-being of his patient during this conversation was giving Lee options, the control to make choices that were important to his quality of life and permission to stop treatment if that was his desire.

Gloria provided support and followed the wishes of her husband. She did not redirect the conversation in an attempt to protect Lee from the reality of the situation. When she provided feedback, she made it clear that she would support her husband's wishes.

Dr. Wright and I conveyed to Lee that there was no right or wrong way to proceed and that his reactions were normal.

Words can be difficult to find when breaking bad news, which is why I have so often compared it to feeling like "walking on eggshells." I used simple but profound words to convey compassion and let Lee know how empathetic we were to his situation.

Earlier I talked about how people often avoid talking to those who are very ill, because they don't know what to say. The same hesitation appears when patients take a turn for the worse. Because you are the caregiver, I encourage you to continue to push yourself to find the words that you're feeling in your heart so you will not regret having missed opportunities to let your loved one know how deeply you care.

Here are some examples of what you and others may want to say to a loved one facing a life-limiting disease who receives bad news:

- "I am sorry and wish that I had better or more comforting words to say, but I can't seem to find any."
- "I am hurting for you and I wish that I could make everything better."

- "I am keeping you in my thoughts and my heart."
- "Is there anything that I can do for you?"

As the caregiver, your loved one's pain and emotions will be experienced by you as well. Your role isn't to be strong all day, every day. As I've conveyed before, from my long experience with patients and their loved ones, I know there will be times when you are exhausted, burnt out and depressed and as the journey draws to an end, this becomes even more typical. Remember to take care of yourself as well as your loved one. Find time to cry and to process your emotions.

Allow others to help you. You are *not* a burden to them; they also are probably feeling like they are "walking on eggshells," wondering how to reach out to you while you are caught between the emotions of caring for a terminally ill person and grieving for what is to come. I believe everyone needs support under these trying circumstances. I want to remind you of the gift that you are giving to your loved one each day: You are making sure that he or she is not taking this journey alone.

Topics for Reflection

1. How have you and your loved one handled hearing bad news? Has it drawn you closer to each other or created distance?

2. Share bad news in order to prevent future regrets.

3. Respect your loved one's feelings and needs after hearing bad news.

4. Communicate often. Not getting regular updates can cause people to speculate, overanalyze and worry about things they probably don't need to worry about. Even if you don't have anything new to report, give at least a weekly update. People crave regular information, even when there's nothing new to report. Share new information as soon as you can.

5. Take the simple but effective approach that open communication is always best.

⁀ Chapter 15 ⁀

Anticipating the End of Life

Preparing for the end of life will differ for each patient and family. When I talk about "end of life," I am referring to the time when the medical team determines that treatments are of no further benefit to the patient. End of life can be defined differently based on each individual's circumstances. For example, a patient may have anywhere from six to twelve months of life left or only weeks, days or hours.

Caregivers and families are often hesitant to discuss the end of life with their dying loved ones because of a number of assumptions:

- He will not be able to handle the news.
- She will give up or lose her will to go on.
- He will get depressed.
- She will think that we are giving up on her.
- He will think that his physician is giving up on him.
- She wouldn't want to upset the children.

Many families prefer to act as if nothing has changed and will encourage their loved one to keep fighting (cheering him or her on, so to speak). Most people who are terminal inherently know when the end is coming, even if those around them attempt to avoid the reality of the situation.

From experience, I believe to avoid the present circumstances is not the best way to handle this very sad period. Both you and your terminally ill loved one will need time to grieve, talk, cry and hug and you cannot get this time back after he or she is gone. I encourage you not to "walk on eggshells" and instead be honest, open and available. I recommend that you follow your gut and your heart.

Ben's Story

Ben was fifty-nine years old and had been battling prostate cancer for four years. He felt hopeful that he would live a long life and that his disease could be kept at bay with ongoing treatments. Each medical visit revealed that he was maintaining "good numbers" and that his disease had not advanced. He felt great and continued to live life as normal.

Ben had been married for thirty-five years and had three grown children and several grandchildren. He was employed as a school teacher and was loved by many. I met Ben and his wife, Maria, during one of his checkup appointments and the tests revealed that his numbers had changed dramatically, meaning that his cancer was growing quickly. I was present when the oncologist, Dr. Lewis, presented this information to them and together we talked about end of life:

> **Dr. Lewis**: I wanted to meet with you today, because
> the lab results are back and there are significant
> changes this time. As you know, we've been able to
> keep the cancer from growing for a number of years,
> but today's report is not good and your cancer is
> growing at a fairly rapid rate based on today's results.
> I know that this must be coming to both of you as a
> shock and I have asked Amy, a social worker, to join
> us today.
>
> We have been using various medications over the
> past several years and they have proven successful,
> but as you know, they were not a cure. Unfortunately,
> I don't have any other treatment options to offer

to you and I think that it is time to discuss shifting gears. I have been upfront with you every step of the way and I will be doing you a disservice if I attempt to sugarcoat the reality of your situation, because you may have important decisions to make in reference to putting your affairs in order.

Ben: I can't believe that I am hearing this today. Are you telling me that there are no further options and that I am going to die soon? How can this be? I feel wonderful; my numbers have been consistently good. It has never even occurred to me that I would die from this cancer. Yes, I am in shock, to say the least!

Maria: I would have to agree with my husband about everything that he just said. Maybe we both misunderstood what the reality of our situation was, because it has never been mentioned that he could die anytime soon. I don't think that you have been up front with us and I am feeling angry and deceived!

Amy: I hear and respect the reactions that both of you are having right now. I think that I would be concerned if you *didn't* have this response. Let me begin by saying that I am sorry that you are receiving this bad news. I can't tell you that I know how you are feeling, but I am able to identify with the immense loss of control that you are experiencing, just as you felt when you were first diagnosed. It must be very scary to hear this information and I want to help to restore some of the ground that you've just lost by giving you some more information.

I am aware of the conversations that have taken place between you and your medical team over the course of your treatment, because I too am a member of that team. I was present when they provided you

with a treatment plan and told you that average survival rates from five to seven years are the norm, but
that the hope was to exceed those odds. I know that it
is probably difficult to remember those conversations
in light of how well things have been going, but the
information was provided to you. It's important that
you are reminded of this fact because I am concerned
that you will use up too much energy if you focus on
feelings of anger and resentment toward your physician. I am not telling you how to feel, but I am hoping
that my input helps to dispel some misconceptions.

Ben: (*tearful*) I don't feel like I am dying. I feel
perfectly well. How long do I have to live? Will
symptoms start to emerge that things are going
downhill? I still can't believe that this is happening
right now. I feel like I am in a bad dream.

Dr. Lewis: I wish that this was a bad dream and if
I could recommend another method of treatment I
would. This is the difficult part of my job. You've asked
some good questions and although I don't have exact
answers, I will provide to you what I have seen over the
years. You have approximately eight to twelve months
to live. During this time period you will become
weaker, have increased lethargy, a loss of appetite and
perhaps some pain throughout your body. There is no
reason that you should remain in pain or discomfort,
because there are medications which can be used to
manage these symptoms. At this time, I would like to
focus on your quality of life. It is my hope that you will
be able to spend quality time at home with your family,
get your affairs in order and even accomplish short
term goals that you may wish to set for yourself. I will
continue to have regular visits with you and would also

like to recommend that Amy set up home hospice to manage your symptoms while you are not here.

Maria: Ben, you have done everything right and there's no way that we could have been prepared for this news. We've been able to make some wonderful memories since you were first diagnosed and will continue to make more with whatever time you have left. If anyone can continue to beat the odds it will be you. Let's stay focused and positive.

Amy: Maria, I agree with you. Ben has done everything right, as have you. I am not here to take your hope away, because I have witnessed things occur that I never thought possible over the years. But I would like to suggest that I help you to plan for the worst case scenario and to hope for the best. Setting up hospice does not mean that Ben only has days to live. Rather, it implies that your physician is not able to offer further treatment at this time and that the disease is not curable. Many people have hospice services for long periods of time and some individuals even discharge their services, because they are doing so well.

Hospice will be able to provide emotional and physical support and is usually covered by insurance. Patients and families receive stellar care at home from nurses, social workers and a medical team. They are also available twenty-four/seven, meaning that if Ben wakes up at 3:00 A.M. and is in pain, you can call the hospice agency and they will send someone over versus having to wait in an emergency room for many hours. Please know that Dr. Lewis will continue to be involved and you can make an appointment to see him at any time.

Dr. Lewis: Everything that Amy said is correct and I couldn't agree more that you both have been and are doing everything right. Further, I am certainly not washing my hands of you and I will continue to give orders to the hospice agency regarding your needs. You are welcome to contact me at any time and we can sort through any issues or problems that may arise.

Ben: I need some time to think about all of this information and I am sorry for attacking you, Dr. Lewis. I was stunned to hear this news today and I am very scared right now. I don't want to be a burden on my wife and I am not ready to leave my family behind. I thought that I would have many more years to spend with them all. But, as you stated, the goals now shift to quality of life, making more memories and living as long as possible. I am relieved knowing that I have longer than a week to accomplish these things and I will make the most out of the next year or longer.

Maria: Ben, you will not be a burden! I love you with all of my heart and I am here for better or worse. Through the years we have supported each other through many difficult times and now is no exception. I know that you would be doing the same for me if things were reversed. As a family, we will get through this together.

Too often patients and families are not provided with the facts about their illnesses until it is too late. In this case, the physician was honest with Ben and Maria about the status of Ben's illness and how much time he had left. Although the physician's news created feelings of loss of control, he was also able to give some back by explaining that there was still time for Ben to do what he felt was important. Additionally, both the physician and I normalized their feelings and provided emotional support. This was vital to "where they were at" and to help them leave the office that day in one piece.

You'll notice that Maria was quick to attempt to "rescue" her husband from the emotional pain. Many caregivers grasp for straws when bad news is delivered, because it is so difficult to witness someone in pain and to feel completely helpless as to how to help them. This response is normal and I worked to gently reframe what the new goals of hope could be going forward while dispelling the myth that Ben could beat his disease.

Hospice services were not mandated and education was gently provided in order to help them decide whether or not they would like to have the services. The concept of "end of life care" was explained in a more understandable tone and stereotypes were dispelled. In the end, Ben was able to accept these services knowing that his oncologist was still going to be involved and that he was not giving up on him. He did not feel like "just a number" but instead, he felt like his doctor truly cared about the relationship that they had built over the years.

Ben and Maria decided to set up hospice services. Ben survived for twenty months, made many more wonderful memories and his wife Maria was at peace knowing that he had the time to live his final months his way.

Handling These Sad Moments

As we have discussed, caring for a loved one who has a life-limiting illness doesn't come with a set of instructions and there is no right or wrong way to feel.

You have every right to want to punch the next person who gets in your way or to scream at people who are smiling and laughing. You have the right to *want* to do these things but *not* the right to *do* these things. There are better solutions for channeling your sadness and anger at the current circumstances. I would like to provide you with suggestions for how to handle these and perhaps future sad moments:

- Call your lifeline. Call that one person in the world who will "get it." It may be your mother, father, sister, brother, best friend or close coworker. Call the person who will let you be vulnerable and will provide you with support.

- Ask to meet privately with the medical social worker. Medical social workers are trained grief counselors and very capable of providing emotional support.

- Attend a support group and/or individual therapy. Both are safe places to express sadness and grief.

- It is also okay to talk to your loved one who has the life-limiting illness. He or she most likely understands your sadness due to the circumstances. You both could use a hug and who better to receive one from?

- Seek support from your church, synagogue or other religious or community group.

- If your children are now adults, share your sorrow with them. They too may need to express their feelings of sadness and you will be providing an opportunity for this to take place.

If hospice has been set up, *please* use the nurses and social workers as avenues to express your feelings. They are some of the most compassionate individuals I have ever met.

We have discussed why caregivers want to protect their loved ones from end of life discussions, but now I would like to focus on you, the caregiver. Perhaps it is not your loved one whom you are protecting. Perhaps you are having difficulty accepting that your loved one's end of life is approaching. You are probably feeling very frightened. Know that you are not alone.

Preparing to let someone go whom you love is painful and the majority of people with whom I work struggle during this difficult time. It is also very normal to experience a disconnect between your mind and your heart when you are told that nothing more can be done medically for your loved one.

Remember how helpless you felt when your loved one was told that he or she had a life-threatening disease? What did you do to compensate for these feelings? You probably placed all your energy into fighting the disease with your loved one. You became more sensitive to his or her needs, wants and wishes. It is now time to shift your focus and to place all of your energy into helping your loved one have a good quality of life for whatever time is left. It is just as important that you and your family (children and others) experience a good quality of life with the loved one. This will be very hard to achieve if you are trying to avoid the reality of the situation.

Topics for Reflection

1. Do you and your loved one fully understand the medical issues at this time? If you don't, I encourage you to make an appointment with your physician to ask more questions.

2. Ask your loved one what his or her hopes and wishes are at this time.

3. Are his or her wishes on paper (i.e., Advance Directive, living will and an actual will)?

4. Does your loved one have unfinished business that he or she wants to attend to, such as visiting with family or writing letters to be left behind?

5. Does your loved one wish to attend services related to his or her faith or talk to someone in the congregation?

6. Loss of control continues to be a primary theme. What *does* your loved one have in his or her control and have you pointed this out to him or her lately?

Chapter 16

What is Hospice and How Do We Talk about It?

You may be asking yourself, *What does it mean to have a good quality of life for someone who is terminal? Is that even possible?* It *is* possible and we will discuss in this chapter how you can assist in this stage of your loved one's illness through the concept of hospice services. Nothing can take away your pain, but I hope the information in this chapter will offer some options that may be available and aid you, if your insurance and/or finances permit and they conform to the wishes of you and the patient.

What is Hospice?

The philosophy of hospice care is to provide quality of life to those who have terminal illnesses. Hospices accomplish this by providing a multi-disciplinary team that consists of nurses, physicians, social workers, home health aides, pharmacists and volunteers. A hospice's primary focus is to prevent and limit physical, emotional and spiritual pain and suffering to the best of the medical team's ability. The hospice staff views the entire family as "the patient" who can benefit from supportive counseling and services.

What Are the Requirements To Be in Hospice?

- A physician indicates that a person has a terminal illness.

- The remaining lifespan of the patient is estimated at six months or fewer (though I have met many patients who have a much longer lifespan in hospice).
- Curative treatments are no longer in use.

I never introduce the concept of hospice unless the patient or family can demonstrate an understanding that they know the illness is advanced and that there are no further curative treatments. This is important for two reasons:

- If the patient and/or family has no idea the patient is terminal and I discuss hospice care, I will alienate myself from them.
- Perhaps the patient and/or family is in denial and could benefit from supportive counseling, which will enable them to become more realistic.

Gary's Story

Presenting the concept of hospice to a patient can be helpful, as Gary's example indicates. I encourage you to share such information with your terminally ill loved one and family.

> Gary, I know that when I first met you your hope was to be cured and I have watched you battle this disease with everything you have. I admire your strength and determination. During our last visit, we discussed the concept of hope and the different stages and phases of it as your disease has advanced. You have told me you are realistic and understand that eventually you will lose your battle with this disease. I am sorry. I wish that I had better words, but I don't.
>
> I would like to share with you that throughout the time we have known each other, you have done everything right. There is nothing that I could have recommended for you to have done differently and I don't want you to look back with regret. Our hope

now shifts to making sure that you have a good quality of life and that you do not suffer. To ensure that,
I would like to set up hospice services, but before I
explain what hospice is, I'd like to acknowledge that
many people feel frightened when they hear the word
hospice. Many fear that it means they must have only
days or hours to live.

I can't see into the future, but it is our goal to
keep you alive for as long as possible. Hospice services provide the best odds of allowing quality time
for you and your family. I feel very strongly that you
should remain in control of what you want, but you
cannot make choices that meet your needs without
knowing your options. I am now going to explain
what hospice is and I encourage you to use the love
and support of your family to help you as well.

Gary, let's take the word *hospice* out of the
equation for now and simply say that I would like to
arrange to have some of the most caring and compassionate nurses assist in your care. Their primary goal
is to monitor your symptoms and assist in providing
a good quality of life. Again, I want to make sure that
you understand your options and that your safety
comes first.

There are three different settings in which this
care can be provided:

Home Hospice: Hospice nurses will come to your
home and do an assessment of what your current
needs are (e.g., ordering medical equipment,
monitoring pain and symptoms). They will make
an ongoing schedule for visits.

I don't want to mislead you, Gary. They do not
take the place of your primary caretakers. Rather,

they add to your support system. Depending on your symptoms, they may only come a few times a week or they may come daily. As your illness advances, they will be in your home more. Although they are not in your home twenty-four hours a day, they are always available and on call. For example, if you wake up at 3:00 A.M. with significant pain, your caregiver can call them. They will be able to handle your needs over the phone or they will come to your home to assist. The goal is to bring the care to your home versus calling 911 and having to stay in an emergency room for hours.

Gary, I know this is difficult to talk about, but I want to make sure that you and your family fully understand the concept of hospice. They will be providing support for your end of life care.

I want you to know that your physician and medical team will continue to be involved with your care even when hospice is involved. If you want to make appointments to continue to see your physician to "check in with him," you can.

I would like to move forward and set up these services for you, with the understanding that you can start or stop at any time. You remain in control of making these choices, but it has been my experience that most people are surprised at the amount of care and support that is offered through hospice.

Gary, I have worked with many people who are receiving care in their homes but who decide for any number of reasons that they would like to obtain their care in a facility. Going to an inpatient hospice is one way to accomplish this. Let me explain what that is:

Inpatient Hospice: I want to convey to you that many people are hesitant or resistant to explore inpatient hospice as an option, because they think I am talking about a nursing home. I am not; rather I am suggesting going to a place that specializes in end of life care. I consider the employees to be some of the most sensitive and caring staff that you could imagine.

The difference between home hospice and inpatient hospice is that the latter provides twenty-four/seven care and support. Your family is welcome to participate with your care as much or as little as they feel comfortable. They may also spend the night at the facility. The atmosphere is much like being in a home environment and the bedrooms are very nice. The hospice physician will continue to update your regular physician.

There is one last setting where hospice services can be provided:

Hospice in Nursing Facilities: There are stand-alone hospices and there are also nursing facilities that have beds that are set aside for hospice patients. In most cases, when a person is receiving hospice care within a nursing facility, an outside hospice agency comes in to provide specialized care to the patient. There are several reasons why you might choose hospice services in a nursing facility:

- There may not be a stand-alone hospice center close to where you live.

- You may know and like a nursing facility close to your house and wish to be there.
- You may feel that it is a better location than home.

Gary, I have never met anyone who would rather be anywhere but home. But there are many families that cannot provide twenty-four/seven support in the home, often because of employment and other responsibilities for children. As you make your choices, I am merely suggesting that you try to look at the entire picture. Since you are doing well physically at this time, one option may be to arrange home hospice now and transition to an inpatient hospice setting should things become more difficult.

Having a Successful Conversation about Hospice

Here are the key points to what was accomplished during my conversation about hospice care with Gary. You can borrow from these themes to use in discussion with your terminally ill loved one:

- Gary's hope was not taken away; rather it was shifted. I reinforced that the primary goal at this and future stages was to address his quality of life and to ensure that he would not suffer.
- Gary again heard that he was terminal and would have time to "put his affairs in order."
- I reinforced that Gary had done and was doing everything right. It is very common that patients question whether or not they "gambled" correctly with the treatment plan provided when they were first diagnosed (e.g., "If I had just gone for that second opinion or tried the natural herbs…").
- I provided all of the options related to hospice settings so that in the future Gary could make choices that meet his needs.

- I reminded Gary that he was in control of the choices I had presented, with the understanding that his safety *must* be the primary focus.
- Many patients think that their physicians will "forget about them" if they enter into hospice. I explained to Gary that his doctor would still check up on him and consult with the hospice staff. Gary could even make appointments to see his physician should he desire.
- I let Gary know that his feelings were normal.

It may be difficult, as the caregiver, to resist wanting to step in and make what you view as the most appropriate and rational decisions for your terminally ill loved one. But remember, there is probably no greater feeling of loss of control than facing one's death. It is critical that the patient be a part of the process and tell you what his or her wishes are. Even if things cannot be arranged the way he or she wants due to realistic safety concerns, you can be at peace knowing that he or she still had the opportunity to voice his or her opinion and wishes.

Topics for Reflection

1. The number one reason that people don't want to accept the help of hospice is the misconception that hospice equals impending death.

2. The reality is that people can have a long time to live and still receive the support that hospice has to offer. Accepting hospice means that there is no cure for the illness and that the focus has shifted to maintaining quality of life.

3. Your children need to be a part of the process and open communication should remain consistent throughout.

4. There are several options available for providing end of life care based on your comfort level and safety concerns: home hospice, inpatient hospice or a nursing home.

5. What supports are available to you for providing care in the home? If you are the only caregiver in the home and have limited external help, I encourage you to talk to a social worker in order to determine what options may be available and whether or not you can realistically handle your loved one's needs in the home.

Chapter 17

Understanding the Physical and Emotional Needs of Your Dying Loved One

A person who is approaching the end of life will have many physical changes. In many cases he or she will have no desire to eat or drink. Most people will grow weaker and spend much of their time sleeping. Family members and caregivers often struggle emotionally as their loved ones' physical statuses decline.

Decrease in Appetite

We are taught early in life that when someone is weak and sick, he or she must eat and drink in order to improve. Remember when you were sick as a child and your mother encouraged chicken soup and other liquids? Many mothers say to their ailing children, "You must eat and drink in order to keep up your strength." It is only natural to think that the same applies when people whom we love are terminal. This strategy doesn't always improve their symptoms and instead can actually make them worse. Forcing food and liquids on a terminally ill patient can cause more discomfort to a person when his or her body is in the process of shutting down. Complications related to a disease are what will cause a terminally ill person to die, not lack of nutrition and hydration.

If you, the caregiver, cannot give nourishment to your loved one at his or her bedside, you may be feeling helpless. You may struggle with immense loss of control. Relinquishing control and watching nature take its course is painful and difficult, but remember that your role has not changed, it has shifted. Your presence each day is allowing your loved one to be at peace knowing that he or she is not alone.

What If My Loved One Wants to Eat?

If your loved one wants to eat and drink, allow him or her to indulge. Make sure that he or she is alert enough to swallow the food and liquid, because if he or she isn't, he or she might choke or aspirate (when food or liquid enters the lungs). Your loved one will probably only eat very small portions, as his or her body will not be able to tolerate large quantities at this point.

Feeding Tubes and Intravenous (IV) Hydration

Many caregivers and families request that feeding tubes and IV hydration be started when their loved ones' appetites and liquid intakes decline. Families have a very difficult time understanding that their loved ones' bodies are shutting down and do not desire these things. Many family members feel guilty, because they incorrectly think that they are starving their loved ones to death.

I am not a physician, but I want to share with you what I have witnessed to be a "good death" after experiencing the process many times with patients and families: The use of feeding tubes and IV hydration is counterproductive to the concept of hospice care. It is widely supported in the medical field that forcing nutrients and liquids into a person's body while it is in the process of shutting down will create discomfort.

You are not causing your loved one pain or suffering by following the cues of his or her body. If he or she could eat and drink, he or she would. For you, the caretaker, this is one more step toward letting go. Your difficult task is to attempt to separate your heart and desires from your loved one's needs as those needs change.

Additional Equipment and Procedures

- **Oxygen:** Many patients acquire a new need for oxygen as they grow weaker, which can be caused by multiple issues such as acquired pneumonia, infections, fluid in the lungs and a host of other possible complications. The levels of oxygen that can be provided vary and some levels cannot be sustained outside of the hospital. If a patient has a critically high oxygen requirement that can't be reduced to a safe level, he or she will most likely pass away in the hospital. Many patients *are* able to leave the hospital even though they need oxygen. It can be administered easily in the home.

- **Pain Medication:** No person should have to endure pain and discomfort. There are specialized pain teams that are dedicated to making sure that the right forms of medications are used for your loved one. Some medications can be taken orally, some administered through a pain patch on the skin and some through an IV, also known as a PCA pump. A PCA pump is typically used when a patient has significant pain and/or is not alert enough to take medications by mouth. Only a trained nurse or physician can change the doses and rate of this pump. If your loved one's pain is not well controlled, alert the medical team and/or hospice staff immediately.

- **Blood Transfusions:** There are various reasons why a patient may require blood transfusions (e.g., the patient can't maintain a healthy level of blood cells due to the disease that he or she has and/or the patient could have an internal injury that can't be operated on because the risks outweigh the benefits) and whether or not to continue to receive blood transfusions is a personal and often difficult choice. When a patient is approaching the end of life, the medical team usually recommends that all transfusions be stopped. The choice is given to remain at home and stop transfusions versus spending long days at the hospital and missing quality time at home. If a patient decides to continue to receive the transfusions, there will eventually come a point of diminishing returns and it will no longer be effective to sustain life. There is no right or wrong choice on this one. It's based purely on the patient's wishes.

- **Medical Equipment:** I let patients and their caregivers know many of the options that exist in reference to medical equipment, because it may make things in the home easier. Please note that I always ask the patient what his or her preference is when it comes to ordering these things, because hearing others' suggestions based on a patient's physical limitations can be very defeating and depressing.

  Examples of equipment:

  - Hospital bed (Sheets don't come with it and two top sheets can be placed over each other, because there are no fitted sheets for hospital beds.)
  - Wheelchair (The patient may have limited mobility or may want to get out of the house.)
  - Bedside commode
  - Rolling walker (This is used by patients to stabilize themselves. Can also be used in the bathtub as makeshift side rails.)
  - Bedside table

Sometimes caregivers and patients are hesitant to order medical equipment, because they aren't sure whether or not they will need it. My suggestion is to order the equipment and the worst that happens is that it sits unused. But should it be needed, it is there! Most equipment is rented and can be returned at any time.

End of Life Care in the Hospital and Preparing for Visits

Not all patients are physically stable enough to leave the hospital. Many prefer to remain in the hospital, because they feel safer knowing that the medical team is monitoring their care. As a clarification, our healthcare system is not set up to have patients remain in the hospital when they are deemed medically stable by a physician and insurance companies will not cover the costs of staying past that point. But when patients are too fragile to move and death is imminent, they meet the criteria to remain in hospital.

During this stage your loved one will most likely be sleeping the majority of the time. Many patients begin to experience shallow breathing and there can often be a significant amount of time that lapses in between breaths. This is the body's natural way of slowing down. Blood pressure and heart rate are much lower at this time.

Some patients exhibit what is known as Cheyne-Stokes respiration, meaning that they look like they are gasping for air and/or are having difficulty catching their breath. Please know that they are not suffering or experiencing air hunger. Again, this is the body's way of shutting down. The physician will arrange to have morphine administered, which will relax the patient's lungs and make breathing easier. In my experience, patients are very close to passing away if this is occurring and are not alert and/or aware of their physical changes.

The medical team will write orders to reflect that a patient is "comfort care" as end of life approaches. This means that there will be no heroic measures taken to save a patient's life should his or her heart stop of natural causes. IV fluids and nutrition will be stopped as well. Again, stopping these things will *not* cause physical discomfort to a person. Studies have shown that a person experiences *more* discomfort when these things are forced into their bodies when their bodies are trying to shut down.

I am giving you an idea of what to expect as you witness the end of life. None of this is easy to experience.

I encourage you to prepare family members and/or other visitors about your loved one's physical status and what they can expect to see when they enter the hospital room. The medical team, nursing staff, clergy and social worker can help everyone cope with these difficult issues.

Each case is different and I reiterate that there are no "shoulds" or "should nots." Whatever decisions you and your loved one make will not, unfortunately, change the final outcome, so follow your gut, heart and the indications from your loved one's body to avoid future regret.

Topics for Reflection

1. Is it difficult for you to resist the urge to force your loved one to eat and drink even when her or she exhibits decreased appetite?

2. Many caregivers ask, "How will I know when my loved one is approaching death?" "You will know" is the most common answer. Your loved one will exhibit noticeable physical changes (e.g., shallow breathing, sleeping more, increased weakness, lack of appetite).

3. Remember to prepare family members and other visitors about your loved one's physical status and what they can expect to see when they enter the room.

4. Are you putting yourself on the "to do list"? You cannot take care of others if you don't take care of yourself.

⋟ Chapter 18 ⋞

What Does Death Look Like?

The circumstances of and reactions to death are different for every individual. In my many years of counseling work, I have met patients and families who were at peace when death came and I have witnessed others who were not.

A question I am often asked by caregivers is: "How will I know when the end is here for my loved one?" People want to make sure that they are present at the bedside during those critical last hours. There are always exceptions, but here are some common signs that your loved one is approaching death:

- His or her breathing slows down.
- He or she has long pauses in between breaths.
- His or her blood pressure drops dramatically.
- He or she is unresponsive.
- His or her skin color becomes pale.

While these changes are visible, I want to assure you that they are not indications of suffering. If you and your loved one have obtained hospice services, this is when hospice staff is involved for longer periods of time and symptoms are monitored very closely to ensure that there is no pain or suffering. It is also during this time when medications such as morphine are introduced or increased. These medications are not used to speed up the end of life; rather they allow the body to relax, which reduces suffering.

What does death look like under these circumstances? It looks like your loved one is sleeping.

Death looks peaceful. I have witnessed many deaths and 99 percent of the time the individuals look as if they are sleeping. The patients that I have been privileged to watch take their last breath have not appeared to be in pain nor were they suffering. Most have been surrounded by their families and loved ones at some point during their final days and many have passed away during the quietness of the night when visitors weren't present.

As was discussed previously, a patient's body begins the process of shutting down in stages. There is lower blood pressure, shallow breathing and a deep sleep. It is usually pretty clear when a terminally ill person is about to pass away, because the blood pressure drops dramatically and breathing slows down. Then breathing stops.

These are the end of life experiences that I have witnessed, but there are other endings to people's lives that are unexpected or not as peaceful. It is important for you to know that sometimes life ends when we aren't expecting it. There can be complications from medications or other conditions in the body that can't be foreseen. This is why I encourage people to prepare their advance directives while they are still healthy.

Patients with Their Own Agendas

There are times when a patient has his or her own agenda for the end of life and decides when he or she is ready to move on.

A very common question caregivers ask me is, "If my loved one is weak and withdrawn, does he or she know that I am present with him or her?" It is my opinion that your loved one does know when certain people are present and it is also my belief that he or she can hear the voices of those around him or her. In my years of experience, I have witnessed numerous unresponsive patients stay alive until the final family member was present and accounted for. Once this occurred, then the loved one passed.

Similarly, I have worked with many families who kept bedside vigils as they waited and anticipated being present for their loved ones' deaths. It was only when these families finally decided to take much needed breaks for fifteen or thirty minutes that the loved ones passed away. In these cases, perhaps the patients didn't want to create more emotional pain for their families, so they waited until everyone left the room.

There are other cases where patients stayed alive, seemingly waiting for what they felt was the right time to die. For example: Joe, a terminal patient, was at the very end stages of life. He knew that Christmas was a few days away and made it his goal to stay alive until December 26, because he didn't want Christmas to be the anniversary of his death. He felt that if it was, his family would always be saddened during what should be a happy holiday. He should not have survived that long, but he did and he passed away the day after Christmas.

If this is your first time grappling with what death will look like, try to accept the peace that results from the end of your loved one's suffering and the good memories of his or her life, which will not be forgotten. Also, remember that as the caregiver you gave that person not only the gift of caring but also of being there during the journey.

Topics for Reflection

1. What has been your experience with death up until this time? What are your beliefs and understanding about the dying process?

2. If you've experienced a loss in the past, what helped you cope during that time? Can you draw from past experiences to help you now?

3. As stated in the prior chapter, there can be noticeable changes when a person is approaching end of life (shallow breathing, loss of appetite, increased weakness, more sleeping). If hospice is involved they will help you during these hours and provide support.

4. Have you and your loved one discussed his or her wishes in reference to having a funeral versus being cremated? These are the types of issues that remain in your loved one's control. If he or she is able to share his or her thoughts with you, as difficult as it may be, remain open to your loved one's needs.

5. Be mindful to keep the children part of the process.

6. Find some peace in the fact that your loved one's pain is over.

Chapter 19

Should Children
Go to Funerals?

A funeral is one of the first reality checks for a child that the world can be complex and scary. You will not be able to shield your child from this reality of life, but if you are able to keep communication open and prepare him or her for what will take place, he or she will learn to experience death and loss in a more healthy fashion.

How Old Should a Child Be to Attend a Funeral?

Children have different needs and reactions to a loved one's death and you will have to make the final judgment based on your child's emotional understanding and maturity level. I think it is appropriate to bring young children to a funeral if they have a basic understanding that things live and die (e.g., they have discussed or learned about life and death at school, church or home, have had a family pet or a relative die). I do not suggest bringing infants to funerals, because they will require extra attention that you or others may not be able to give and they will not have any concept of what is going on around them.

Preparing a Child to Attend a Funeral

Continue to be open and honest with your child and adjust your responses and vocabulary according to your child's age and understanding.

What is a funeral?

It is difficult to have this kind of discussion with your child, but it is vital that he or she understands what he or she is about to view and experience. Here is an example of what you might tell your child:

> A funeral is a place where we and other people who
> knew and loved Daddy will come together to say
> goodbye. His body will be placed in a wooden box
> called a casket. He will not be in any pain, because
> he is not alive. Remember when I explained to you
> what death is? His spirit has left his body and he
> cannot breathe, see or feel. His skin and bones go
> underneath the ground and will become part of
> nature. That is why the casket will be lowered into the
> ground. I will have a special stone made that will have
> Daddy's name on it. This is called a gravestone and
> we can come visit Daddy's grave, see the stone with
> his name and remember him.

What do people do at a funeral?

Explain to your child what to expect to see and hear from the other people present at the funeral. It is important to warn your child that the people around him or her will be emotional, to prepare your child for your own display of emotions and to give him or her permission to show his or her emotions. An example of how to explain this to your child:

> There will be people around you at the funeral who
> will be crying, because they are sad, like we are, that
> Mommy died. It is okay if you cry or don't cry. I know
> that I will cry, because I am sad, but I want you to
> know that I am okay. It is normal to show sadness.

Will I see a dead body?

If a child is too young to be able to make a choice about whether or not he or she wants to see the loved one's body in an open casket, then it may be best not to have the child see it. If the child is capable of this decision (approximately age five or older), then explain to him or her ahead of time what the body will look like, reinforce that the loved one is not alive and give him or her the choice of whether to view the body. In either case, follow your instincts and be aware of your child's emotions and coping skills.

What happens after a funeral?

If you will be having people visiting your house or going somewhere for a remembrance after the funeral, explain to your child that people often gather after a funeral:

- To celebrate the loved one's life. For example, "Daddy would want us to be surrounded by the people we know and who love us."
- For the family of the deceased to receive support from others.

Let your child know that it is okay if he or she feels like having a good time, because his deceased loved one would want him or her to be happy. Also allow your child the space to be alone and feel sad if those are his or her needs.

Helping Your Child Grieve

The age and maturity levels of children whose loved ones die are different. Younger children may act out or exhibit behaviors that are not characteristic of them. They will have a difficult time "finding their words" and will show their feelings through actions. Older children and teens may want more time alone or experience a drop in grades at school. They may also act out, become angry and hostile and have difficulty expressing themselves.

These are signs that children are grieving. I recommend getting the school counselor involved and alerting your child's teachers to the loss that your family has experienced. You and these professionals can help your child put his or her feelings into words. Through time and consistent support, your child will pass through this phase of grief. If your child appears to be stuck for longer than six to eight months, you may want to seek a therapist who works with children. There are also grief support groups for children depending on the age of your child.

For older children, a therapist or support group may be beneficial, but do not force your child to go to counseling at this point. Here is an example of how you may broach the topic:

> I know that it's been hard since Dad died and I hurt for you. I wish that I could bring him back, but I can't. I think that you might feel a little better if you talked to someone about how all of this is making you feel.
>
> When I hold all of my sadness and anger inside, I eventually feel like I am going to explode. I think what you are experiencing is normal. I would be *more* concerned if you were acting like everything is just fine. I am your parent, though, and I worry about you. I can find you a group of other teens or a counselor to talk to. Either one will give you the space to get things off your chest with people who understand and care. Take some time to think it over. I will support whatever you want to do.

Discussing the death of his or her loved one lets your child know that you are "tuned in" to his or her emotions and are supportive of his or her needs. It also provides an avenue to model how to deal with feelings in a healthy way. This example also addresses the negative stigma that people often feel when mental health options are offered. It is important to let your child know that he or she is allowed to experience these emotions. Stating, "I would be *more* concerned if you were acting like everything is just fine" validates to your child that the grief and emotions with which he or she is struggling are normal.

This may be your child's first experience with grief and loss and it is common for people, not just children, to think that the intense pain they are feeling in the moment will never go away.

Here are examples of what you may want to say:

- "I know how much pain you are in right now. Your heart hurts and you may think that it will never get easier, but I promise you that it will. As time goes on, you will begin to feel less pain and the days will be easier to get through."
- "I know from my own heartbreaks and losses that things do get better. I can't tell you a specific timeframe for when the world will feel a bit brighter, I can only reassure you that it will. I am not telling you to forget your mother or that we are moving on without her, because no matter how much time goes by, she will live forever in your heart. We can talk about her whenever you'd like."

Anniversary Dates

The first year after your child's loved one passes away will be particularly difficult, especially around anniversary dates (e.g., birthdays, holidays, vacations and Father's or Mother's Day). Often, most people struggle with these and so too will a child. Open the door for communication and reassure him or her that you are available for talking and support.

Ignoring your loved one's death during what should be festive occasions or holidays will only intensify the feelings. Set an example for your child and express that you miss your loved one and wish that he or she could be with you on this day.

Also, you may use this opportunity to reminisce, tell stories to remember the good times that you all shared together and laugh. Your loved one may be physically gone, but he or she is still very much present within the hearts of those who loved him or her.

Moving Forward

It is my belief that our children often compel us to make it through the next minute, hour and day after a loved one dies and it may become unclear who is really helping whom when facing a loss. You may think that you are doing what's best for your child by getting out of bed each day, but by doing so, you too are taking small steps toward healing and moving on. When certain days feel unbearable, I encourage you to seek comfort through self-care and support resources. Remember, you are not alone and there are people in your life who are eager to assist you however they can. Reach out to them.

Topics for Reflection

It is best not to confront children with information that they may not yet understand or want to know. As with any sensitive subject, we must seek a delicate balance that lies somewhere between avoidance and confrontation, that encourages children to communicate. That isn't easy to achieve. It involves:

- being sensitive to their desire to communicate when they're ready;
- not putting up barriers that may inhibit their attempts to communicate;
- offering honest explanations when you are obviously upset;
- listening to and accepting their feelings;
- not putting off their questions by telling them they are too young;
- giving brief, simple answers that are appropriate to their questions; answers that they can understand and that do not overwhelm them with too many words.

This may sound easy or perhaps intimidating. Be gentle with yourself and remember: You don't have to have all of the answers, but you do have to be present.

Chapter 20

After Your Loved One Dies

I want to convey to you who are reading this book because a loved one has died that I am sorry for your loss, the difficult journey you've been on and the challenging path you still face. There will be people (perhaps your loved ones, friends or coworkers) who will say things that they think are supportive, but aren't. For example:

- "Time heals all."
- "This was God's will."
- "He's in a better place now."
- "I know exactly how you are feeling."

Their words may make you feel angry or resentful, but try to remember that people mean well when they try to express their condolences, even if they do so in awkward ways.

Nobody will ever be able to understand your loss and pain. It is unique to you. Try to keep in mind that your friends and coworkers may feel, as you did when you faced the sadness and pain of your loved one's illness and death, that they are "walking on eggshells" around you and may feel helpless as to how to comfort you. Simple is often better and, from your own experience now, one day in the future when someone you know experiences a loss you will be able to convey this clearly: "I am sorry and I am hurting for you."

What to Expect

You have been the primary caregiver and it may be difficult to return to the life you knew before, now that your role has ended. In the beginning, there will probably be a wealth of external support offered by family and friends. Take it in, feel it and let others take care of you, because this support will trickle away in time. People have busy lives and must return to them. That leaves you alone, still grieving and still trying to figure out how to pick up the pieces and move forward.

As much as you may want to move on, your internal system will resist. It is in shock and it will not let you forget that it too requires nurturing. Early on you may feel like the world is going on around you (almost as if everyone is in slow motion) and that you are not attached to it. It is normal to experience a sense of anger and to ask, "How can people be going about their normal, everyday affairs when I am in so much pain? How can they be smiling and laughing?"

The Seven Stages of Grief

First proposed by Dr. Elisabeth Kubler-Ross, many therapists share her belief that there are different stages of grief and that a person experiencing a loss may go back and forth between these stages for a period of six to eight months or longer.[6] No two individuals experience grief in the same way. The seven stages of grief model will, I hope, provide a general guide for what to expect:

- **Shock and Denial:** Hearing a physician say that your loved one has passed can create a physical and/or emotional reaction that is often difficult to describe. At that instant, everything around you seems to stop existing and your entire body and mind feel blank. Numbness and disbelief may lead you to deny the reality of the situation in an attempt to avoid dealing with it practically and emotionally.
- **Pain and Guilt:** Emotional pain can be crippling and is often one of the strongest emotions that human beings experience.

It's like a deep cut and must be attended to and worked through in order to find some relief. The pain felt when someone you love has died is often accompanied by feelings of guilt, for example: *Why didn't I spend more quality time with her?* or *If only I had been nicer when we disagreed.*

- **Anger and Bargaining:** When someone you love dies, anger is a very normal and prominent feeling. People often feel angry at the world, their faith, family and friends. Many people wonder, *How can everyone walk down the street with smiles and laughter when I am in so much pain?"*

  In this stage many people feel desperate and they will attempt to make emotional bargains in order to make the situation better. For example: "Please, if you bring back my wife I promise to never take another drink of alcohol for as long as I live."

- **Depression:** Grief and loss for your deceased loved one can become more than you may be able to bear. Your physical and emotional ability to continue forward slows or halts. You may feel paralyzed with an overwhelming sense of sadness and perhaps even hopelessness.

- **The Upward Turn:** You are less numb and more capable of feeling life around you. The future is foreseeable and physical and emotional symptoms of grief lessen.

- **Reconstruction and Working Through:** As your mind and heart begin to heal, the problems of everyday life become more manageable. You reorganize your life without your loved one.

- **Acceptance and Hope:** Time *can* make things more manageable. It may not seem possible that you will ever experience joy or a sense of inner calmness again, but you will. This stage brings the acceptance of the reality of your loved one's passing. The pain of your loss will come and go, but there will be movement forward as well. Each day forward will bring the hope for a better tomorrow.

Finding a Safe Place to Grieve

Your mind and spirit have been on autopilot for a long time. Your system needs time and space to grieve.

As you move forward it is appropriate to seek support from your family and friends. But, as mentioned earlier, they too have lives to attend to and stressors of their own. They love and care about you, but they will not be able to provide the consistent support you will need.

I encourage you to find a local support group or individual therapist. Each has its own unique set of benefits and if you can do both, I recommend it. You may contact your local hospice for information related to bereavement support groups, as well as churches and synagogues, medical information services and such Web sites as Findatherapist.com.

Support Groups

A support group allows you to be surrounded by others who have undertaken journeys similar to yours and who can relate to the feelings that you are experiencing. You will come to realize that you are not alone.

Therapy

For months you have had to repress some of the difficult emotions you were feeling and forge ahead. A therapist provides an avenue for you to express yourself.

Venting your painful feelings with a professional counselor is very valuable. At first it can be painful to explore all of the feelings that surround the loss that you are experiencing, but if you persevere, my hope is that you will emerge with a greater sense of self and freedom.

Finding a therapist who meets your needs may take some investigation. You may have to try several therapists before you find "the right fit."

How Long Should You Be in a Support Group or Therapy?

Individuals vary in the amount of time they need to participate in support groups or individual therapy. Some quickly reach a point where they feel they have taken several steps forward and at other times they may feel they have taken several steps backward. This is normal. Be aware that many have found therapy beneficial and that there is hope of reaching a consistent inner calmness.

Will I Ever Feel Happy Again?

You are probably questioning whether or not you will ever feel joy and happiness again in your life. I believe that you will. Grieving serves a purpose and, unfortunately, time is a large obstacle to contend with right now. On the days that feel impossible to get through, take a moment to sit and take a few deep breaths. I also recommend that you allow yourself to have a good cry.

Guilt for Moving On

Many caregivers feel a sense of guilt when they notice actual movement forward or feel a glimmer of happiness. They feel like they are betraying their deceased loved ones and fear forgetting them.

You are not betraying your loved one by moving forward or by experiencing happiness. Rather, you are doing what he or she would have wanted you to do. You will not forget your loved one or replace the love that you have for him or her. Neither of you had control over your loved one's death. Now your job is to live. Reenter life as your emotions permit.

Topics for Reflection

1. Which stage are you in regarding your grief? Do you feel "stuck" within a particular stage? If so, remember that the passage of time may make things more manageable.

2. It may be hard to get back to "normal" life now that your caregiving role has ended. Seek the support of family, friends and outsiders.

3. Seek professional help if you have signs of severe depression, anxiety or other symptoms mentioned in this chapter.

Chapter 21

Reentry

Have you ever watched a space shuttle make its reentry into the Earth's atmosphere? It is one of the most amazing sights that I have ever witnessed. There is much anticipation, concern for those on board and sheer excitement when it lands. The fact that a space shuttle can rise above the sky millions of miles away and then come back safely is exciting and wondrous.

Think of the space shuttle's astonishing reentry as similar to your reentry into the everyday life routines of you and your family after the death of your loved one.

Circumstances beyond your control took you to what felt like millions of miles away from life as you knew it. After handling the caretaker role you assumed for your loved one, you can now concentrate not only on issues which arose for others in your personal life, but also those you could not attend to regarding your own well-being. Make this a savoring time for those around you, now that your life and theirs are normal and close once again.

Life as you knew it is now changed forever. You have been through your own private journey to which most others will not be able to relate. That doesn't mean they don't care; it simply means that you are walking a different path. This will also be a time for new beginnings and your options may appear narrow right now, but there are actually many opportunities available to create change.

Ways to Get Back into Life

- Join groups and associations that spark an interest for you. For example, many people get involved with groups that raise money and support the illness that their loved ones passed away from (e.g., American Heart Association, breast cancer awareness groups, American Cancer Society). This may help you to feel that the loss of your loved one was not in vain and that you are honoring his or her memory by fighting for a cure.

- Get connected or reconnected with a church, synagogue, etc. Most caregivers are not able to attend to their spiritual needs while taking care of a terminally ill loved one and now you will have time to rededicate to this area of your life.

- Cultivate a hobby. There is rarely enough time in the day to attend to our creative sides and/or hobbies. What are some of yours? I encourage you to explore at least one of the interests that you come up with. You deserve to do joyful things!

- Revitalize your job situation and visualize new horizons. Up until this point in your life things most likely have been pretty chaotic and attempting anything new at work was most likely placed last on your list. Spend some time thinking about where you want to go from here (in reference to your job). Do you want to advance or perhaps change jobs altogether? Now is the time to explore new ways to stimulate your brain and to attend to new or prior goals.

- Work on personal issues. We all need "tune ups" or have unresolved issues that nag at our inner cores. Use this time to sort through some of your "stuff" with a therapist and/or support group. It can be very helpful!

- Take a holiday. When was the last time that you took a day just for you? I call them "me" days and try to schedule them once every few months. These are days that are set aside to do whatever *you* want to do. Personally, I find shopping to be quite therapeutic, but you may enjoy having lunch with a friend, getting your hair done, relaxing at a spa, playing a round of golf or simply sitting in a quiet space and reading your favorite book. If you have children at home, please do not use them as an excuse to put off your holiday. Do *not* feel guilty about taking care of yourself!

- Join exercise and adventure groups. These can be stimulating, are a good way to socialize and can get you out of the house. Maintaining an exercise routine can be difficult, but joining a group can make things easier and fun. And you *will* feel better (mentally and physically) afterwards for doing it.

You will still miss your loved one and hold onto fond memories of him or her. There will continue to be unexpected sad moments that will catch you off guard. But be glad for those around you and cherish your time together. If certain days feel unbearable, reread previous chapters to find sources of comfort and keep in mind that you are not alone.

I am very proud of you for continuing to move forward even though there were and will be times when you didn't and won't think you can.

As you continue your reentry, please do not feel guilty about all of the love and support that others provided to you, whether others watched your children, made you meals or just sat with you. They do not want you to feel in debt to them.

Pay forward the kindness that friends and family showed you in your time of need to others. You are not the same person you were prior to your loss; you now have so much more compassion and wisdom to share with others in need. Giving to others when your heart permits will help in your continuing healing process.

Topics for Reflection

1.   Are there aspects of your life that were "put on hold" because of your loved one's illness? Did you neglect your physical or spiritual self-care, as some do when they assume the role of caregiver?

2.   When was the last time you took a day just for yourself? If it has been a while, reward yourself and move on.

3.   Sad moments may occur from time to time, as will fond memories of your loved one. This is to be expected.

4.   Remember to "pay it forward," that is, to repay the love and support you received by doing good deeds for others in need.

⁓ Appendix ⁓

Obtaining Additional Support

Support Resources for Caregivers

After Giving
www.aftergiving.com

Allscripts Care Management
Headquarters:
222 Merchandise Mart Plaza
Suite 2024
Chicago, IL 60654
Toll Free: 1.800.654.0889
www.extendedcare.com

American Cancer Society (ACS)
Toll Free: 1-800-227-2345
TTY: 1-866-228-4327
www.cancer.org

Caregiver Community Action Network (CCAN)
www.nfcacares.org/connecting_caregivers/caregiver_community_
action_network.cfm

Caregivers Network
67 Water St.
Suite 105
Laconia, NH 03246
Phone: 603-528-6945
Toll Free: 1- 866-634-9412
E-mail: caregivers@metrocast.net
www.caregiversnetwork.org

CareGiving
Phone: 773-343-6341
E-mail: denise@caregiving.com
www.Caregiving.com

Caring Connections
HelpLine: 800.658.8898
Multilingual Line: 877.658.8896
E-mail: caringinfo@nhpco.org
www.CaringInfo.org

Coping with Loss and Grief
Dr. Weide
Virginia:
801 N. Pitt Street
Suite 113
Alexandria, VA 22314
703-548 3866

Maryland:
6917 Arlington Rd.
Suite 223
Bethesda, MD 20814
240-229-1893
E-mail: grief@earthlink.net
www.coping-with-loss-and-grief.com

Exceptional Parent Magazine
Subscription Customer Service and New Orders:
Toll Free: 800-372-7368
E-mail:wsheehan@eparent.com
www.eparent.com

Family Caregiver Alliance
180 Montgomery Street
Suite 900
San Francisco, CA 94104
Phone: 415-434-3388
Toll Free: 800-445-8106
www.caregiver.org

Find a Therapist
www.Findatherapist.com

National Association of Social Workers (NASW)
750 First Street, NE
Suite 700
Washington, DC 20002
Phone: 202-408-8600
www.socialworkers.org

National Caregivers Library
901 Moorefield Park Drive
Suite 100
Richmond, VA 23236
Phone: 804-327-1111
E-mail: info@caregiverslibrary.com
www.caregiverslibrary.org

National Family Caregivers Association
10400 Connecticut Avenue
Suite 500
Kensington, MD 20895-3944
Toll Free: 1-800-896-3650
Phone: 301-942-6430
E-mail: info@thefamilycaregiver.org
www.nfcacares.org

Seniors Site
Seniors-site.com

Today's Caregiver
3350 Griffin Road
Ft. Lauderdale, FL 33312
Phone: 954-893-0550
Toll Free: 1-800-829-2734
E-mail: info@caregiver.com
www.caregiver.com

Well Spouse Association
63 West Main Street
Suite H
Freehold, NJ 07728
Phone: 732-577-8899
Toll Free: 800-838-0879
E-mail: info@wellspouse.org
www.wellspouse.org

Caregiving Resources

Aging with Dignity/Five Wishes
PO Box 1661
Tallahassee, FL 32302
Phone: 850-681-2010
Toll Free: 888-5WISHES (888-594-7437)
E-mail: fivewishes@agingwithdignity.org
www.agingwithdignity.org

Alzheimer's Association
National Office:
225 N. Michigan Ave, Fl. 17
Chicago, IL 60601
Phone: 312-335-8700
TDD: 312-335-5886

24/7 Helpline:
Phone: 1-800-272-3900
TDD: 1-866-403-3073
E-mail: info@alz.org
www.alz.org

American Association for Retired Persons (AARP)
601 E Street, NW
Washington, DC 20049
Toll Free: 888-OUR-AARP (888-687-2277)
TTY: 877-434-7598
Spanish: 877-MAS-DE50 (877-627-3350)
E-mail: member@aarp.org
www.aarp.org

American Diabetes Association
ATTN: Center for Information
1701 North Beauregard Street
Alexandria, VA 22311
Phone: 1-800-DIABETES (1-800-342-2383)
E-mail: AskADA@diabetes.org
www.diabetes.org

American Heart Association National Center
7272 Greenville Ave.
Dallas, TX 75231
Phone: 1-800-AHA-USA-1 (1-800-242-8721)
E-mail: Review.personal.info@heart.org
www.heart.org

American Lung Association
1301 Pennsylvania Ave, NW
Suite 800
Washington, DC 20004
Phone: 202-785-3355
E-mail: info@lungusa.org
www.lungusa.org

Arthritis Foundation
PO Box 7669
Atlanta, GA 30357
Phone: 800-283-7800
www.arthritis.org

CiteHealth
Corporate Office:
945 N 5th Ave
Brighton, CO 80603
Citehealth.com

GrowthHouse
2261 Market Street
#199A
San Francisco, CA 94114
E-mail: info@growthhouse.org
www.growthhouse.org

Hospice Foundation of America
1710 Rhode Island Ave, NW
Suite 400
Washington, DC 20036
Phone: 202-457-5811
Toll Free: 800-854-3402
E-mail: hfaoffice@hospicefoundation.org
www.hospicefoundation.org

Johns Hopkins Kimmel Cancer Center
The Harry and Jeanette Weinberg Building, Ste. 1100
401 North Broadway
Baltimore, MD 21231
Phone: 410-955-5222
www.hopkinsmedicine.org/kimmel_cancer_center
Videos online: http://www.youtube.com/user/
JohnsHopkinsKimmel#grid/user/22EC27BDF57C677F

Make-A-Wish Foundation
4742 N. 24th Street
Suite 400
Phoenix, AZ 85016
Phone: 602-279-WISH (602-279-9474)
Toll Free: 800-722-WISH (800-722-9474)
www.wish.org

Muscular Dystrophy Association
National Headquarters:
3300 E. Sunrise Drive
Tucson, AZ 85718
Phone: 1-800-572-1717
E-mail: mda@mdausa.org
www.mdausa.org

National Association for Home Care and Hospice
228 Seventh Street, SE
Washington, DC 20003
Phone: 202-547-7424
E-mail: hospice@nahc.org
www.nahc.org

National Kidney Foundation
30 East 33rd Street
New York, NY 10016
Phone: 212-889-2210
Toll Free: 1-800-622-9010
www.kidney.org

National Multiple Sclerosis Society
New York National Office:
733 Third Ave., 3rd Floor
New York, NY 10017

Washington, DC National Office:
1100 New York Ave., NW
Suite 660
Washington, DC 20005

Denver National Office:
900 South Broadway
Suite 200
Denver, CO 80209
Phone: 1-800-344-4867
www.nationalmssociety.org

National Stroke Association
9707 E. Easter Lane
Suite B
Centennial, CO 80112
Phone: 1-800-STROKES (1-800-787-6537)
E-mail: info@stroke.org
www.stroke.org

Pediatric Oncology Resource Center
E-mail: porcwebmaster@pfeist.net
www.ped-onc.org

Transverse Myelitis Association
Sanford J. Siegel, President
1787 Sutter Parkway
Powell, OH 43065
Phone: 614-766-1806
E-mail: ssiegel@myelitis.org
www.myelitis.org

Care Homes/Homecare

Assisted Living List
Assisted-living-list.com

Assisted Senior Living
E-mail: ken@assistedseniorliving.net
www.assistedseniorliving.net

Brandywine Senior Care, Inc.
Corporate Office:
525 Fellowship Road
Suite 360
Mount Laurel, NJ 08054
Phone: 856-813-2000
Toll Free: 1-877-4-BRANDY (1-877-427-2639)
www.brandycare.com

ElderCarelink
190 Front Street
Suite 201
Ashland, MA 01721
E-mail: contactus@ElderCarelink.com
www.ElderCarelink.com

Hospice
401 Bowling Avenue
Suite 51
Nashville, TN 37205
E-mail: info@hospicenet.org
Hospicenet.org

International Association for Hospice and Palliative Care
5535 Memorial Dr.
Suite F--PMB 509
Houston, TX 77007
Phone: 936-321-9846
Toll Free: 866-374-2472
www.HospiceCare.com

Midwest Palliative & Hospice CareCenter
Robert H. and Terri L. Cohn Campus
2050 Claire Ct.
Glenview, IL 60025
Phone: 847-467-7423
www.carecenter.org

National Hospice and Palliative Care Organization
1731 King Street
Suite 100
Alexandria, VA 22314
Phone: 703-837-1500
E-mail: nhpco_info@nhpco.org
www.nhpco.org

A Place for Mom
Corporate Headquarters:
1300 Dexter Avenue North
Suite 400
Seattle, WA 98109
Phone: 206-285-4666
Toll Free: 1-877-MOM-DAD9 (1-877-666-3239)
E-mail: advisor@aplaceformom.com
www.aplaceformom.com

Senior Living
E-mail: ken@seniorliving.org
www.seniorliving.org

Sunrise Senior Living
International Headquarters:
7900 Westpark Drive, Suite T-900
McLean, Virginia 22102
Phone: 703-273-7500
www.sunriseseniorliving.com

Special Needs Trust

Conservatorship, Trusts and Wills
www.empowermentzone.com/conserve.txt

Good Shepherd Fund Special Needs Trust
1641 N. First St
Suite 155
San Jose, CA 95112
Phone: 408-573-9606
Toll Free: 888-422-4904
www.goodshepherdfund.org/needs.html

National Special Needs Network
4613 North University Drive
#242
Coral Springs, FL 33067
Phone: 561-447-4152
E-mail: jminde@comcast.net
www.nsnn.com

SeniorLaw: Supplemental Needs Trusts
www.seniorlaw.com/snt.htm

SSI & Trusts - EM-00067
http://www.nosscr.org/ssas/ssitrust.htm

Financial Help and Insurance Issues

Assurant Health Short Term Medical
Phone: 800-394-4296
www.assuranthealth.com/corp/ah/HealthPlans/short-term-health-insurance.htm

COBRA Insurance
www.COBRA-Insurance.com

The Family and Medical Leave Act
www.FMLAOnline.com

No COBRA
27 Lazurite
Suite 100
Rancho Santa Margarita, CA 92688
Phone: 949-713-7222
Toll Free: 866-NO-COBRA (866-662-6272)
E-mail: info@nocobra.com
www.NoCOBRA.com

Partnership for Prescription Assistance Program
Phone: 1-888-4PPA-NOW (1-888-477-2669)
www.pparx.org

Rx Assist
E-mail: info@rxassist.org
www.rxassist.org

Social Security Disability Insurance (SSDI) Applications
Myler Disability
PO Box 127
Lehi, UT 84043
Toll Free: 800-816-0822
E-mail: disabilityclaim@ssdisabilitylawcenter.org
www.SSDisabilityApplication.com

Direct Financial Aid

Andre Sobel River of Life Foundation
PO Box 361460
Los Angeles, CA 90036
Phone: 310-276-7111
E-mail: info@andreriveroflife.org
andreriveroflife.org

Cancer Fund of America, Inc.
2901 Breezewood Lane
Knoxville, TN 37921
(800) 578-5284
E-mail: info@cfoa.org
www.cfoa.org

Childhood Cancer Interest Groups
www.ped-onc.org/ccorg.html

Kelly Anne Dolan Memorial Fund
P.O. Box 556
602 S. Bethlehem Pike, Bldg. D, 2nd Floor
Ambler, PA 19002
Phone: 215-643-0763
www.kadmf.org

National Children's Cancer Society
1 South Memorial Drive
Suite 800
St. Louis, MO 63102
Phone: 314-241-1600
www.thenccs.org

National Transplant Assistance Fund
150 N. Radnor Chester Road
Suite F-120
Radnor, PA 19087
Phone: 610-727-0612
Toll Free: 800-642-8399
www.ntafund.org

The Szott Foundation
PO Box 211658
Eagan, MN 55123
E-mail: info@szottfoundation.org
www.szottfoundation.org

UnitedHealthcare Children's Foundation
MN012-S286
PO Box 41
Minneapolis, MN 55440
Phone: 952-992-4459
www.uhccf.org

Government Agencies

Centers for Medicare & Medicaid Services
7500 Security Boulevard
Baltimore, MD 21244
Phone: 410-786-3000
TTY: 410-786-0727
Toll Free: 877-267-2323
TTY Toll Free: 866-226-1819
www.cms.gov

Supplemental Security Income, SSI
Office of Public Inquiries
Windsor Park Building
6401 Security Blvd.
Baltimore, MD 21235
Toll Free: 1-800-772-1213
TTY Toll Free: 1-800-325-0778
www.ssa.gov

Fundraising

Sparrow Clubs USA
906 NE Greenwood Ave.
Suite 2
Bend, OR 97701
Phone: 541-312-8630
E-mail: info@sparrowclubs.org
www.sparrowclubs.org

Notes

Chapter 6

[1] Maryland Department of Health and Mental Hygiene, "Medical Care Programs Eligibility," http://mmcp.dhmh.maryland.gov/SitePages/Medical Care Programs Eligibility.aspx.

[2] Julie M. Whittaker, "Social Security Disability Insurance (SSDI) and Medicare: The 24-Month Waiting Period for SSDI Beneficiaries Under Age 65," Congressional Research Service, http://assets.opencrs.com/rpts/RS22195_20050714.pdf.

[3] American Cancer Society, "ACS Mission Statements," http://www.cancer.org/AboutUs/WhoWeAre/acsmissionstatements.

[4] Patty Feist, "Financial Help and Insurance Issues," http://www.ped-onc.org/cfissues/financehelp/finhelp.html.

Chapter 7

[5] National Family Caregivers Association, "Connecting Caregivers," http://www.nfcacares.org/connecting_caregivers/.

Chapter 20

[6] Jennie Wright, "7 Stages of Grief: Through the Process and Back to Life," Recover from Grief, http://www.recover-from-grief.com/7-stages-of-grief.html.

Acknowledgements

The message of *The Oprah Winfrey Show* on November 11, 2009, resonated with me. Although I had heard Oprah Winfrey's message, "The only failure to trying is to not try at all" so many times before, it was on this day that I fully acknowledged its impact and felt it in my soul. This idea pushed me forward to follow my dreams despite having insecurities.

From that day forward, I made a commitment to Ms. Winfrey, to myself and to caregivers of loved ones to write this book for all the caregivers I have known and those whom I haven't yet met who confront the issues of caring for a loved one with a life-threatening disease. I feel immense gratitude toward those who supported and believed in me along the way.

A special "thank you" to my parents who have always supported and encouraged me to follow my dreams. I could not do the work that I do without having had a good foundation. My ability to "hold" others during their times of need is a result of the values that I was raised with.

I have had opportunities provided to me which have been building blocks for where I am today and I will be forever thankful to my parents for providing these avenues to me. Finally, writing a book is no small task and there is a lot of rejection and risk that goes hand-in-hand with this journey. My upbringing has afforded me a strong sense of self to endure this road and to forge ahead when perhaps others may have given up. I thank my parents for instilling these qualities in me.

Louise Knight, Michael Hibler and Laurie Singer provided support, guidance and spirit-lifting cheers throughout this process. They never questioned or doubted my vision. Instead, they walked the journey with me and never looked back.

A special thank you goes to Dr. Benjamin Carson, who took on the task of reviewing this book without hesitation, despite a very hectic schedule. His support and feedback were invaluable.

I thank Nikki Heuer, who typed day and night to place my handwritten words into manuscript form. Her sore fingers were a true reflection of unconditional support.

Barry Miller, who typed, copied, mailed, cried and laughed with me throughout the process, I thank you!

My appreciation goes to Penelope Cordish, aka "Aunt Penny," who gifted me her personal time to edit this book.

Thank you to Patrick Mullen and Greg Rubin, who pushed me beyond my limits and kept me "centered."

Unbounded thanks go to my childhood friend, Lisa Williams, who cried with support when I shared my ideas. She made the vision feel attainable.

I am indebted to all of the patients and their families who allow me into their worlds during what must be one of the most painful times they will ever endure. I will never take these encounters for granted.

I thank Morris Wiley for believing in me. He is a rare breed within the education system and *I can't* is not part of his vocabulary. I hear your voice of encouragement still.

I am indebted to all of the people who provided encouragement along the way. Particularly I thank my colleagues at Johns Hopkins, the neighbors in "The Hood" and Karen Donovan.

I would like to thank Dr. Joan S. Dunphy, publisher and editor-in-chief at New Horizon Press, who took a risk on accepting this book for publication knowing that the marketplace was already crowded with this topic. Further, she was able to appreciate the need for support toward caregivers and understood that what they need most is a simple yet profound way to know that they are not alone on their journey of caring for someone who has a terminal disease. Thank you for believing in my vision to help others.

I would additionally like to thank several other valued staff members at New Horizon Press who played a key role in turning my original self-published book into an expanded version of support to others: Joanna Pelizzoni (editor), who carefully crafted new areas of interest to be placed into this book and her sense of humor and support when I lost many hours worth of work on my computer; Charley Nasta (production editor), who has spent many hours correcting errors, editing this book and overseeing the production from start to finish; and JoAnne Thomas (vice president of special sales and marketing), who has been involved since day one with the initial contract and ongoing marketing. It takes a "team" to create a good product and I have been very fortunate to have people of such high quality encourage and assist me along the way.